Good Practice Guide: **Extensions of Time**

RIBA Good Practice Guides

Other titles in this series:

Negotiating the Planning Maze, by John Collins and Philip Moren (2006)

Keeping Out of Trouble, by Owen Luder, 3rd edition (2006)

Employment, by Brian Gegg and David Sharp (2006)

Painless Financial Management, by Brian Pinder-Ayres (2008)

Fee Management, by Roland Phillips (2008)

Good Practice Guide:
Extensions of Time

Gillian Birkby, **Albert Ponte** and **Frances Alderson**, Fladgate LLP

RIBA ⫘ **Publishing**

© Gillian Birkby, Albert Ponte and Frances Alderson, 2008
Published by RIBA Publishing, 15 Bonhill Street, London EC2P 2EA

This is a revised edition of the book *Construction Companion to Extensions of Time*, written by Gillian Birkby and Paul Brough, which first appeared in 2002 published by RIBA Enterprises Ltd.

ISBN 978 1 85946 298 0

Stock Code 64213

The right of Gillian Birkby, Albert Ponte and Frances Alderson to be identified as the Authors of this Work has been asserted in accordance with the Copyright, Designs and Patents Act 1988.

British Library Cataloguing-in-Publication Data
A catalogue record for this book is available from the British Library.

Publisher: Steven Cross
Commissioning Editor: John Elkington
Project Editor: Anna Walters
Editor: Alasdair Deas
Designed by Ben Millbank
Typeset by Academic + Technical, Bristol
Printed and bound by MPG Books, Cornwall

While every effort has been made to check the accuracy of the information given in this book, readers should always make their own checks. Neither the Authors nor the Publisher accept any responsibility for misstatements made in it or misunderstandings arising from it.

RIBA Publishing is part of RIBA Enterprises Ltd.
www.ribaenterprises.com

Series foreword

The *RIBA Good Practice Guide* series has been specifically developed to provide architects, and other construction professionals, with practical advice and guidance on a range of topics that affect them, and the management of their business, on a day-to-day basis.

All of the guides in the series are written in an easy-to-read, straightforward style. The guides are not meant to be definitive texts on the particular subject in question, but each guide will be the reader's first point of reference, offering them a quick overview of the key points and then providing them with a 'route map' for finding further, more detailed information. Where appropriate, checklists, tables, diagrams and case studies will be included to aid ease of use.

RIBA Good Practice Guide: Extensions of Time

Deciding upon what is a fair and reasonable extension of time is one of the most difficult tasks in administering a contract, regardless of which form of contract is used. Unless there is only one cause of delay, separating the numerous simultaneous activities typical in a project is a complex process, compounded by the occurrence of concurrent delays and overlapping problems. As projects become larger and more complicated, many architects are beginning to look to computer-based systems as the means of arriving at appropriate extensions of time. Of course, the success of such an approach still depends on the quality of both the information used and the records kept.

In examining how to assess an extension of time, this guide looks at the basic considerations relating to delays and the factors to be taken into account. It offers pointers as to where and how the necessary information may be found and also explains when and how liquidated damages may be applied. A separate section considers extensions of time under the NEC suite of contracts, which is becoming increasingly popular.

This guide is essential reading for all architects and contract administrators faced with problems of delay, extensions of time and liquidated damages. It will help them be fully aware of all the issues at stake as well as the legal framework which underlies the contracts and under which they must be resolved.

Sunand Prasad
President, RIBA

Preface

Partnering and supply chain integration are now well established in the construction industry. They are intended to bring projects in on time, among other things. Not everyone runs their contracts using these techniques though, and delays still occur on all types of contract, for a variety of reasons.

In this guide we look at the basics of delay, extensions of time and liquidated damages. We consider these from first principles, so it is a useful introduction for those who are not familiar with the process.

We have concentrated on the clauses in the JCT forms of contract that deal with extensions of time, as these forms are the ones most frequently used in the construction industry. However, we have provided a separate chapter on the NEC forms in recognition of their increased use. We consider some of the ethical issues that arise in dealing with extensions of time. We look at some of the difficult problems that can arise for an architect administering these contracts, by way of worked examples, drawing on our legal expertise. Previous versions of the guide were written with Paul Brough, who provided a technical insight into the analysis of delay. Sadly, Paul has since died.

We have written the book from the perspective of the law of England and Wales, as at February 2008. The references to JCT forms are to the 2005 forms. However, in recognition of the possibility that JCT 1998 forms may in some instances still be in use, we have included references to the main relevant clauses on liquidated damages in Section 2, *Liquidated damages*. For further information on the relationship between the 1998 and 2005 forms we recommend the JCT guides to the forms, which include a Table of Destinations showing the 1998 and equivalent 2005 numbering of the clauses.

References to the NEC forms are to the 3rd Edition, first published in 2006.

Gillian Birkby, Albert Ponte and **Frances Alderson**

June 2008

About the authors

Gillian Birkby is head of Fladgate LLP's construction group, a dedicated unit comprising ten fee earners who are experienced in acting for consultants, employers, contractors and subcontractors. Gillian is named as a 'Leading Individual' in Chambers and Partners 2008 *Guide to the Legal Profession* and has extensive experience of advising architects, contractors and employers on the interpretation and administration of construction contracts and in particular extension of time clauses. She also drafts and negotiates the full range of appointments and contracts, as well as assisting in resolving construction disputes. Gillian lectures widely and writes frequent articles for the press on construction topics.

Albert Ponte is a senior member of Fladgate LLP's construction group. He has worked in construction law throughout his career and in recent years has focused solely on contentious matters. His work has involved him in a range of dispute resolution processes and procedures from mediation to adjudication, and the county court to the Court of Appeal. In that time he has pursued and defended a number of claims relating to delay and extensions of time of varying size and complexity.

Frances Alderson is a Partner in Fladgate LLP's construction group. She is listed as a leading practitioner in the *International Who's Who of Business Lawyers* and is the author of a chapter on construction insurance and a chapter on construction in the UK compared with construction in other worldwide jurisdictions. She lectures widely, particularly on the use of the New Engineering Contract. Frances has over 25 years' experience advising employers, contractors and consultants, both producing contract documentation and also resolving disputes.

Acknowledgements

Our thanks go to Mark Chandler of Norman Rourke Pryme, who has kindly updated the technical material in this book, to our colleagues for their valued advice, and to our faithful secretary, Jo Rowden.

Contents

Section 1
Basic principles

In this Section:

- *Who decides on the initial contract period? When can the works commence? What happens at completion?*
- *Does the extension of time clause always apply? Time at large. Making time of the essence*
- *What if the contractor fails to complete on time? Are there any rules about how progress is to be made during the works? What if the contractor wants to finish early?*
- *Liquidated damages*
- *Does a subcontractor have the right to work to a fixed programme?*
- *Domestic subcontractors. Named subcontractors*

Introduction

Time is one of the three crucial elements of a construction contract. The other two are quality and cost. A perfect project would be carried out on time and within budget and be of high quality. It is commonly said, however, that whereas two out of those three can often be achieved, three out of the three cannot. Because of the complexities involved in a construction contract, and in particular the many different trades and professions that are commonly involved in them, construction projects are susceptible to considerable pressure on the 'time' element.

The difficulty is that the parties to a construction contract may have conflicting aspirations. Both employer and contractor can usually maximise their potential profit on a project if completion can be achieved early. The sooner the building is finished, the sooner it can be occupied by the employer, or let in order to generate rental income. The sooner the contractor can move people and materials off site, the greater their profit will be where they are working to a fixed-price contract (the most common situation) and the sooner they can begin to earn money on another contract. However, if the project runs into delay for any reason (which is also common) the parties are immediately in potential conflict. The employer will want to offset the costs of their inability to occupy or let the building; the contractor will want both more time to complete and to be paid for the extra expense caused by the delay.

Prevention principle

The prevention principle provides that where one party to a contract has, by any act or omission, prevented the other party from performing a particular obligation under the contract, they cannot insist upon the performance of that obligation by the other party. Therefore, where an employer is responsible for any delay to the project (referred to as an *'act of prevention'*) they cannot hold the contractor to the previously agreed date for completion unless the contract states otherwise.

If there is no written contract between the parties, the position can be unfavourable to the employer. If, in those circumstances, the project suffers delay due (either entirely or in part) to any act or omission of the employer, the prevention principle means that they cannot insist on completion by the agreed date. Unless the terms of any oral contract to the contrary can be proved, the contractor merely has an obligation to complete within a reasonable time, and the employer has no means of forcing the pace. The employer could make time of the essence

See: Making time of the essence, page 10

but often it is not a good idea to do so. If there is a contract, however, it can contain a mechanism by which time can be managed effectively for both parties. This mechanism is the *extension of time* clause.

The extension of time clause works in the following way. Assume that the contract specifies a fixed date for completion. If the contractor fails to complete by that date, they are liable to pay so-called *liquidated damages* to the employer. This compensates the employer for the contractor's delay.

However, there may be delay to the project that is not 'at the risk of' the contractor: that is, not something for which the contractor has taken on responsibility (typically an act of prevention by the employer such as a variation to the works). In this case, the contractor can apply for an extension of time to complete, if the contract allows for this (the employer's right to liquidated damages is then preserved, but postponed by the length of the extension granted). Liquidated damages are covered below (see page 15) and in Section 2.

If there is no extension of time clause, the contractor may claim that time is at large and that they have the obligation only to complete within a reasonable time. If time is at large, the employer will lose any right they might have had to liquidated damages. Time at large is explained below.

See Does the extension of time clause always apply? Time at large, page 9

If the contract, unusually, states that 'time is of the essence' a different set of rules apply.

See Making time of the essence, page 10

Time of the essence

Making 'time of the essence' in a contract means that if the contractor fails to complete on time the employer can say that the contract is at an end and sue for damages for the contractor's failure to complete on time.

The extension of time clause therefore sets out which of the parties takes the risk when there is delay on a construction project for a particular reason. If the employer takes the risk of that delay, an extension will be granted; if the contractor takes the risk, it will not be.

As highlighted by the judge in *Multiplex v. Honeywell* (2007), extension of time clauses exist for the protection of both parties. The contractor benefits in that time can be extended for completion of the project where they are not responsible for any delay that has occurred, while the employer can proceed safe in the knowledge that they will not fall foul of the prevention principle in the event that they cause any delay.

This guide focuses on the extension of time clause in more detail, and in particular on how that clause works in the JCT forms. There is also a chapter on how extension of time operates under the New Engineering Contract (NEC).

First, however, the points introduced so far are expanded through a brief look at the basic shape of a construction contract.

Who decides on the initial contract period?

Most construction projects have two phases: the *design* and the *work on site*. Early in the design phase a decision should be made about the appropriate form of construction contract. Before the tender documents are sent out, the time period needed to complete the project should be assessed. This is usually done by the quantity surveyor and the architect, who try to come to a realistic assessment, based on the design itself and on their experience. The client, of course, is likely to want an early date for completion.

The information about the length of the construction period is sent out to contractors as part of the tendering process. The aim of this process is to provide contractors with information about the project on which to base their price. It is good practice to have the contract agreed and executed, with the date for completion inserted, before work on site begins. The contract will usually set out either a date for completion or the length of the construction period.

The contractor will also usually be informed at the tender stage of the anticipated date for starting work on site. This, together with the contract period, will be important in calculating the tender sum, because of the need to assess possible rises in the cost of labour and materials and to ensure that both can be made available at the appropriate dates.

A reasonable time period should be set for completing the works. If the period is short considering the amount of work to be done, the employer should expect the tenders submitted to be higher, and quality standards may also suffer.

In practice, the design phase will generally overlap with the construction phase. In recent years, in particular, there has been an increase in the use of contract forms that are *fast track* (that is, which shorten the overall period from starting design work to practical completion), and this is generally achieved by over-lapping the design and construction phases. This does, of course, leave the problem that speed is not always compatible with quality, and it is certainly not compatible with tight financial constraints. Even where traditional forms are used, such as SBC2005, design and construction will often overlap, which can cause delay to the contractor.

When can the works commence?

Once a contractor has been selected, they will need possession of (or at the very least access to) the site in order to start work. Where the work is to be carried out in sections, they may only be given possession of those parts of the site that relate to the first section. Where the contract is carried out in phases or sections, the date on which the contractor is expected to start each of the phases or sections should also be recorded. See Section 2, page 20 for further discussion of sectional completion.

Deferring possession

Under the JCT forms, apart from MW2005 and MP2005, the employer is entitled to defer the contractor's possession of the site for up to 6 weeks beyond the contractual date of possession. In MP2005 the contractor is given access but not possession.

Where the project is notifiable under the CDM Regulations (likely to last more than 30 days or involve more than 500 person days on site), work cannot start on site until the client, as defined by the Regulations (usually the employer), has agreed that the construction phase plan is ready and there are suitable welfare provisions in place, as required by Schedule 2 of the CDM Regulations. It is now therefore more likely than in the past that the date of possession will be recorded as part of the administration of the CDM Regulations.

It is important not to commit the employer contractually to a start date until the construction phase plan and welfare facilities are, in fact, ready. The start date can be stated in the contract as ' [date X] or the date on which the construction phase plan is ready for work to start on site and the Schedule 2 requirements have been met, whichever is the later'. The contractor is responsible for preparing the construction phase plan and organising welfare facilities, and should therefore take the risk that they may not be ready on time. This can be achieved, in the example above, by calculating the date for completion by reference to date X, and not to the date on which the contractor actually starts work on site, if delay in producing a satisfactory construction phase plan and non-compliance with Schedule 2 is the reason why the start on site is later than anticipated.

The tender information should state the date on which it is anticipated that the contractor can gain possession of the site.

The date on which the employer is ready to give possession can be later than the date in the tender documents for many reasons: for example, failure to obtain the necessary planning permission or delays in the tendering process. This is part of the reason why contractors usually state in their tender that it is open for acceptance for a certain number of weeks.

If the date of possession is later than the date given in the tender documents, the actual date of possession should be recorded.

The date of starting on site may be important for various reasons. The date for completion may be calculated by reference to the commencement date (for example, the contract may state that completion shall be 'X weeks from commencement on site'). Also, the operation of the extension of time clause usually depends on an undisputed initial contractual date for completion.

The date of possession should also be distinguished from the date on which off-site work commenced, such as prefabrication or the ordering of long delivery items.

It is quite common for the contractor to be allowed on site 'early' in order to set up site huts, etc. and, again, it is helpful if there is some record of whether this period is to be considered part of the contract period.

Ideally, the construction phase plan (if the project is notifiable under the CDM Regulations) should be ready some days before work is due to start on site. The contract can then be completed with the date for possession inserted, and the contract documents signed by both parties before work starts on site. This ideal is not always achieved. The work on site might start on the basis of a letter of intent or it might just start without either a signed contract or a letter of intent. It is good practice to have, at the very least, a letter of intent before work starts on site, and preferably a signed contract. If there is a letter of intent, the architect should check whether any start date set out in that document is the same as the date on which work actually started on site. If the dates are not the same, or if there is no date in the letter of intent (or no letter of intent at all), the architect should make sure that a written record is made of the correct date. This can either be by letter or in the minutes of the next site meeting. It is important that the date is recorded as soon as possible after work has started on the site, to avoid arguments later on.

What happens at completion?

> ### *Contract administrator*
>
> Most of the JCT forms refer to the person administering the contract as 'the architect' or 'the architect/the contract administrator'. In this guide the term 'architect' is used. In DB2005 the employer's agent undertakes the functions of the architect in relation to extensions of time, unless the employer has said that the employer will carry out this function, so references to the architect include the employer (or the employer's agent) for those functions under DB2005. In MP2005, the employer's representative is similarly entitled to carry out all the employer's functions, and references to the architect include the employer and the employer's representative under that form.
>
> There will of course be circumstances where the architect will not be appointed to provide a 'full service' and their role will not include that of contract administrator. Nevertheless, the architect should still be aware of 'time' and programming issues as they will still be relevant in other respects, such as the timely provision of information.

The completion date is the date on which the project should in fact be ready for handing over to the employer. The architect will inspect the work and issue a certificate or statement of practical completion, which indicates that the work is substantially complete and the building can be handed over to the employer. This is a significant point in the construction process and can give rise to much contention, because it can affect the contractor's liability for liquidated damages: see *Liquidated damages*, page 15 and Section 2.

> ### *Practical completion*
>
> There is no definition of this term in the JCT forms, nor in most other contracts. Judges, for example in *H.W. Nevill v. Wm Press* (1981), have attempted to give some guidance. In that case Judge Newey said that it meant there were only 'very minor de minimis works' still to be carried out, and no visible defects. The JCT forms make no reference to the use of snagging lists of works outstanding at practical completion, yet such lists are almost invariably compiled. Despite what Judge Newey said, the phrase is usually understood to mean that the work is sufficiently complete

to allow the employer to take possession, either to occupy the building or for the purposes of fitting it out, and that there are only minor snagging items left to complete, which can be carried out while the employer is in possession. If the employer, or the architect with the employer's agreement, intends that practical completion will be interpreted differently from the usual standard, for example that completion will not be certified until a somewhat higher standard is reached, or until certain items have been fully completed, this should be made clear in the tender documents and the building contract.

For present purposes, the main significance of the completion date is that it indicates that the time allowed for the construction period has been fixed: the contractor will either pay liquidated damages if the date is missed, or apply for an extension of time under the contract if it is likely to be missed (or both).

The basic rule is that if the contractor fails to complete by the completion date, the employer has a remedy against the contractor in liquidated damages (see Section 2).

If, however, the employer is responsible for, or has taken the risk of, events that delay completion of the works, then in order to preserve the right to liquidated damages for any delay apart from employer's risk items, the contract gives the architect the power to grant extensions to the time period specified for construction. The contractor will not be liable to pay liquidated damages during the period for which an extension of time has been given (see Figure 1.1).

FIGURE 1.1: *Impact of extension of time on liquidated damages (LDs)*

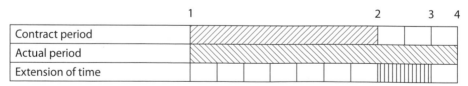

Notes

Period 2 to 3   No LDs in this period because an extension of time has been granted.

Period 3 to 4   Contractor is liable to pay LDs because work is still not completed and no extension of time has been granted.

The circumstances in which such extensions of time are commonly granted under the JCT forms are set out in Section 3.

Does the extension of time clause always apply? Time at large

The employer and contractor do not always fix the time for the construction period in the way explained above. If there is no contractual obligation to complete by a certain date, the contractor's only obligation is to complete the works within a reasonable time, which leaves the employer at risk in terms of meeting any other deadlines that depend on the completion of the works. In these circumstances, time is said to be *at large*.

There are also other occasions when time is said to be at large. For example, where some event has occurred during the course of the contract that is not at the contractor's risk and causes delay to completion but which the extension of time clause does not deal with, time will be at large, and any extension of time clause cannot be used. In this case, if the event in question can be classed as an *act of prevention* by the employer (such as delay in granting possession of the site), its effect will be to invalidate the completion date. If an event does not fall within the terms of the extension of time clause, the architect cannot grant an extension, and the contractor is then under an obligation merely to complete within a reasonable time (*Peak v. McKinney* (1970)). Contractors who are already in delay may look for opportunities to claim that time is at large, thinking that it may assist them, although it may not necessarily do so.

Completion within a reasonable time

In *Shawton Engineering v. DGP International* (2005) the court said that what was a 'reasonable time' in this context 'had to be judged as at the time when the question arises in light of all relevant circumstances'. The relevant circumstances are likely to include any previously agreed completion date in the contract, the full extent of the work including any variations and any other delays that were not within the contractor's control. If the contractor is already in delay because of events that are at the contractor's own risk, such as breakdown of plant, those delays will not be taken into account in calculating the reasonable time for completion.

Example

The maximum period of delay in granting possession of the site to the contractor, under those JCT forms that allow it, is 6 weeks beyond the date of commencement set out in the contract.

- The employer delays granting possession for 7 weeks, which delays the contractor by the same period.
- The architect has no power under the contract to grant an extension of time beyond 6 weeks.
- If the parties do not amend the contract by agreeing a new possession date and a new completion date, time would arguably be at large and the contractor would be required only to complete within a reasonable time.
- This is the legal position even though common sense would suggest that the completion date should be extended by 7 weeks to allow for the delay in commencement on site, with a possible adjustment to the contract sum to reflect later completion.

It should be noted that under the JCT forms (except MW2005) an extension of time for the extra 1 week of delay can be granted under the sweep-up clause – any other impediment or prevention by the employer (see *Any impediment, prevention or default by the employer*, page 34).

Making time of the essence

The time for performance of a contractual obligation can be made *of the essence* by putting express words to that effect into the contract. If this has been done in relation to the date for completion, the contractor *must* complete by that date (subject to any entitlement to extensions of time). Failure to do so will mean that the employer is entitled to treat the contract as a whole as having been *repudiated*. This means that the employer has no obligation to carry out their own part of the contract, and may make a claim in damages.

Repudiation

This term denotes a party behaving in a way that shows they no longer intend to be bound by the contract. This can be by breaching a fundamental term, or *condition,* of the contract (such as the obligation to complete by a specified date where time has been made of the essence) or in some other way depriving the 'innocent' party of substantially the whole benefit which it was intended they should obtain from the contract. If the 'innocent' party accepts the repudiation, they are relieved of the duty to carry out their future obligations under the contract, and can recover damages from the repudiating party.

A construction contract will normally contain an extension of time clause and a liquidated damages clause. This will imply that time is not of the essence in relation to the contractor's obligation to achieve completion by a certain date, because alternative mechanisms for dealing with delay have been adopted.

However, where there is no extension of time mechanism in the contract or it has become inoperable, the employer may wish to make time of the essence as a means of regaining control over the time of completion. If, in those circumstances, the employer believes that the contractor is in breach of their obligation to complete within a reasonable time the employer has the option of either:

1. giving reasonable notice making time of the essence, or
2. treating the failure to complete within a reasonable time as a repudiatory breach.

The latter is an inherently riskier approach for the employer and so making time of the essence is usually to be preferred.

If the employer wishes to make time of the essence, they should serve notice on the contractor requiring completion by a certain date, and – provided this is properly worded and the specified date is reasonable in all the circumstances – it will have the effect of making time of the essence. The notice should be clear and state unambiguously that failure to complete by that date will entitle the employer to terminate the contract. However, any employer considering taking this step should be advised that if the contractor challenges a subsequent termination of the contract, the employer will have the burden of proving that, at the point that the notice was issued, the contractor was in breach of the obligation to complete within a reasonable time. Making time of the essence should not, therefore, be undertaken lightly and should only be considered after careful thought has been given to the possible consequences.

There are various other reasons why time is not usually made of the essence:

- It will usually be quicker and cheaper to allow the existing contractor to finish the work, albeit late, than to employ another contractor who will not be familiar with the works.
- If the works are completed by another contractor, the original contractor's responsibility for parts of the works, and their liability for defects, could be difficult to enforce, because of the 'interference' by the replacement contractor.
- In most construction contracts, the employer already has a remedy in liquidated damages if the contractor is in delay (provided that the contractor cannot show that the employer has committed any acts of prevention).
- There are many cases where practical completion is not achieved by the completion date, but it is not clear at that point whether the contractor may be entitled to further extensions of time. It would be premature for the employer to allege that the contractor's failure to complete by the completion date was a repudiation of the contract. If time had been made of the essence, the employer could accept non-completion as repudiation, but the architect, an arbitrator or the court might subsequently decide that a further extension was due. The employer would then find that they themselves were guilty of repudiating the contract and that the contractor was entitled to damages for repudiation.

The JCT forms, with their provisions for extensions of time and liquidated damages, are designed to avoid these problems by making it unnecessary for time to be of the essence.

What if the contractor fails to complete on time?

The consequences for a contractor who fails to achieve practical completion by the completion date, described in this section, were set out by the House of Lords in *Percy Bilton v. GLC* (1982) as follows:

- The general rule is that the main contractor is bound to complete the work by the date for completion stated in the contract. Failure to do so will leave the contractor liable for liquidated damages to the employer.
- That is subject to the exception that the employer is not entitled to liquidated damages if by their acts or omissions they have prevented the main contractor from completing their work by the completion date.
- These general rules may be amended by the express terms of the contract.

The House of Lords' judgment here neatly summarises the purpose of the extension of time clause: it preserves the employer's right to liquidated damages, and is therefore for the benefit of the employer, as well as the contractor.

Are there any rules about how progress is to be made during the works?

Under most contracts, although the contractor will usually have a completion date to which they are working, there is a great deal of flexibility in determining the order of work and the exact timing of each individual element. The contractor's obligation is usually limited to the requirement that they should commence the works on the date of possession and thereafter proceed 'regularly and diligently', using their best endeavours to avoid any delay, however it might be caused. If they do that, and complete on time, they will not be in breach of contract even if they do not in fact adhere to their own programme. The exception to this is if their programme is one of the contract documents. Where the JCT forms are used unamended, the programme is not a contract document (except for the design programme in MP2005). However, in NEC forms the programme is a contractually binding document (see Section 9).

It follows that if the timing of the different parts of the works results in added expenditure to the employer, for instance by entitling the contractor to higher rates to reflect increased costs for work carried out later in the contract period, the employer can do nothing about this, and must pay the extra costs incurred. Sometimes employers attempt to control this by making payments on the basis of construction *milestones* being achieved, rather than on a monthly basis. These milestones can be events such as completion of piling, achieving watertightness or end of first fix electrical work.

> ### *Example*
>
> The firm Cleveland Bridge were employed to manufacture, supply and install the gates and gate arms for the Thames Barrier. The contract set out certain key dates by which various parts of the works had to be completed, and Cleveland Bridge complied with these. At the same time, the employer had to pay more in fluctuations for inflation costs than anticipated, because of the sequence that Cleveland Bridge had adopted for the different parts of the works. The court held that this was not a breach of contract. Cleveland Bridge were entitled to organise the progress of the works as they saw fit (*GLC v. Cleveland Bridge* (1986)).

What if the contractor wants to finish early?

Another common feature of a contractor's programme is that it will show that the contractor plans to finish the work early: that is, before the date for completion. The question then is whether the architect is obliged under the construction contract to supply information, supplementary drawings, etc. in such a way as to enable the contractor to achieve early completion.

> ### *Example*
>
> This issue was raised in *Glenlion Construction v. The Guinness Trust* (1987). This concerned a JCT1963 contract for the construction of a residential development for the Trust. Glenlion were required by the bill of quantities to provide a programme showing a completion date 'no later than the date for completion'.
>
> A dispute arose, and the court said that Glenlion were entitled to complete before the date for completion and to carry out the works in order to achieve that earlier date. There was, however, no parallel obligation on the architect to provide information to enable the contractor to achieve this early date. If there had been, this would have had the effect of imposing on the employer an earlier date for completion.
>
> Although in some circumstances an employer might welcome early completion, it might equally cause difficulty, for example if funding arrangements had been made on the basis of a longer programme.

Liquidated damages

'Liquidated damages' is the term used to describe the sum (that is, a liquidated amount) that the parties have agreed by contract will be payable where one of them is in breach of contract. (The damages will be *unliquidated* where the figure is not set out in the contract or cannot be calculated from its terms, and has to be assessed by a court or arbitrator.) Generally, the contract will specify a weekly or daily sum that is to be paid or deducted for the period after the completion date has passed until practical completion is achieved.

Further information on liquidated damages is given in Section 2.

Does a subcontractor have the right to work to a fixed programme?

The position of subcontractors on construction contracts is particularly difficult, since they must co-ordinate the timing of their own work with that of the main contractor and other subcontractors. This can result in delay to the project since, subject to the terms of the subcontract, there is no general duty to comply with a contractor's programme. Contractors often put wording in a subcontract stating that the subcontractor must comply with the contractor's requirements as to timing.

Examples

- Kitsons were the insulation subcontractor for Matthew Hall for the construction of Terminal 4 at Heathrow. The order from Matthew Hall stated: 'Works should be carried out in accordance with the dictates of our site management team, to enable the overall mechanical services to be completed and handed over to our client on 18.3.85.' Matthew Hall were obliged to secure availability and access to site areas so far as they were able. Kitsons were late in completing their work and said that was because Matthew Hall had failed to make work available as required by the revised programme. Matthew Hall refused to grant an extension of time. The judge said that both parties must have understood that there was little chance of working closely to a programme and that as long as Matthew Hall tried to obtain access to areas that were needed by Kitsons for their own work, Mathew Hall were not in breach of contract even if Kitsons were sometimes unable to do any work at all because of lack of access and as a result failed to comply with the revised pro-gramme (*Kitsons v. Matthew Hall* (1989)).

- A piling subcontractor claimed for the cost of some piling work they carried out. The main contractor counterclaimed for loss caused by the subcontractor's delay in carrying out the work. The subcontract provided that the subcontractor was under an obligation to complete the sub-contract works and to use their best endeavours to prevent delay in the progress of the subcontract works. The judge held that this did not require the subcontractor to plan their work to fit in with the contractor's work or to finish any part of the subcontract works by a particular date so that other parts of the works could proceed. The exact wording of the contract was crucial (*Pigott Foundations v. Shepherd Construction* (1993)).
- A sub-subcontractor carried out the design and installation of a control system for a research facility for British Nuclear Fuels, but there was no contract with the subcontractor, as the parties could not agree on the programme. The court said that there is no duty to comply with the main contractor's programme where this is not a contractual require-ment, but that there *is* a duty not to interfere unreasonably with the work of other trades. This amounts to an obligation to be aware of the other trades and to co-operate with efficient working practices so far as this is consistent with the subcontractor's own legitimate commer-cial interests (*Serck Controls v. Drake & Scull Engineering* (2000)).

A subcontractor can put the whole programme in delay. If this happens, the consequences for the contractor and the subcontractor will depend on the exact terms of the various contracts.

Domestic subcontractors

Contractors who have engaged a domestic subcontractor are entirely liable for them and are not entitled to an extension of time on account of the domestic subcontractor's delay unless that delay falls within one of the express categories set out in the extension of time clause in the main contract, or the contract otherwise allows it. The extension of time clause in a subcontract should be *back to back* (that is, consistent) with the equivalent clause in the main contract, otherwise problems may be caused for either the subcontractor or the contractor. The named specialists referred to in MP2005 are also the entire liability of the contractor, even though there are restrictions, as their title suggests, on who can be engaged as a named specialist.

Named subcontractors: IC2005 only

The position of named subcontractors under IC2005 is slightly different. Where the main contract provides for work to be carried out by a named subcontractor, the provisions of Schedule 2 of IC2005 will apply in respect of that subcontract. Schedule 2 provides that where the employment of a named subcontractor is terminated either because of insolvency or default, or with the consent of the architect, the contractor will be entitled to an extension of time if they suffer delay as a result.

SUMMARY

- Time, together with quality and cost, are the three crucial elements of a construction contract. It is therefore essential to agree realistic dates for commencement and completion of the works.
- The dates for commencement and completion of the works can be fixed dates or can be set by reference to related events (e.g. completion within 10 weeks after commencement).
- Where a contractor fails to complete the work by the completion date the employer may be entitled to claim liquidated damages.
- Where delay is caused by an event for which the contractor is not responsible, an extension of time clause will provide for the extension of the completion date, thus reducing the contractor's liability to liquidated damages.
- If there is no mechanism for extending time under the contract, in the event of delay for which the contractor is not responsible or at risk, the completion date will fall away and time for completion of the works will be 'at large'.
- If time for completion is at large, the contractor is only under an obligation to complete the works within a reasonable time.
- Time for completion can be made 'of the essence' by putting words to that effect into the contract or, where time is at large, by giving reasonable notice.
- Failing to complete on time where time has been made of the essence can be a repudiatory breach of contract which entitles the 'innocent' party to terminate.

Section 2
Liquidated damages

In this Section:

- *Definition and purpose*
- *Partial possession*
- *Comparison with 'penalties'*
- *Calculation of LDs*
- *The JCT forms*
- *Procedure for levying LDs*
- *Contractor's delay*
- *Other standard forms*

Definition and purpose

Liquidated damages (also known as LDs) are the compensation payable for breach of contract for which a method of calculation has been agreed in the contract. They must be a genuine pre-estimate of the loss that the employer will suffer on breach of contract by the contractor. In a construction contract they are used most often for the contractor's failure to achieve practical completion by the completion date, and should be expressed as a daily rate for delay. That rate will apply from the day after the completion date until practical completion is achieved. LDs therefore act as an encouragement to the contractor to complete on time, because the contractor knows precisely what the consequences will be, in monetary terms, of failing to do so, and that the employer will usually have the right to deduct the liquidated damages from any money due to the contractor.

> ### Sectional completion
>
> Where there is sectional completion there should be a separate figure for liquidated damages for each section. There must also be a date for completion, or a method of calculating the date, for each section. Previously, JCT contracts had either a sectional completion supplement or sectional completion modifications, both of which required additions to the Appendix to deal with this. The JCT forms (with the exception of MW2005, which does not have provisions for sectional completion) incorporate the sectional completion provisions into the various forms. *It is essential* that the Contract Particulars are properly completed if sectional completion is to apply and it is advisable to delete the relevant recital if there is to be no sectional completion.

Liquidated damages clauses are generally worded so that the parties know in advance the sum that is payable if there is a delay to completion caused by a breach of contract by the contractor, thus avoiding the need to sue the contractor for damages for delay. This assists both the employer and the contractor by sparing the expense of adjudication, litigation or arbitration over the amount of damages payable.

Delay in completion for a reason that is the contractor's risk is a common feature of construction projects, and a liquidated damages clause means that the contractor knows what they will have to pay the employer in those circumstances. The contractor can then decide whether it is worth taking steps to accelerate the works at their own cost to reduce the delay in reaching practical completion.

The 1998 JCT contracts referred to 'liquidated and ascertained damages'. The term currently used in the JCT forms is 'liquidated damages'. Liquidated damages are ascertained by reference to the rate set out in the Contract Particulars which replace the Appendix of the JCT contracts, and are found near the front of the form after the Articles (except MP2005, where the Contract Particulars are at the back of the form following the operative clauses).

> ### *Rate of LDs*
>
> It is better to state a daily rate, because a weekly rate could be seen as a penalty (see *Comparison with 'penalties'*, below). It is common to express the rate as '£x per week or part thereof', which again could constitute a penalty, unless the employer's losses for a delay of part of a week are the same as for a whole week of delay. Alternatively, a weekly rate could be understood as allowing the employer to claim LDs for full weeks of delay only, and not part weeks. Instead of a daily rate the rate could be expressed as '£x per week and pro rata for part of a week'.

Partial possession

The JCT forms, apart from MW2005, allow the employer to take partial possession of some of the works before there has been practical completion of the works or a section of them. This can be done only with the contractor's consent. For instance, if the employer has an item of plant to be used for their business, and which they wish to have delivered to site on a certain date, they may agree with the contractor that they will take possession of the area where the plant will be installed. Obviously, in those circumstances it would not be right for the employer to continue to levy LDs for the whole of the works if the contractor does not complete by the completion date. There is therefore a provision in the contract for the architect to assess what proportion of the works has been taken into the employer's possession, and to apportion the LDs figure accordingly.

It is quite easy for the LDs provisions to go wrong where there is partial possession, unless the JCT forms are left unamended and the Contract Particulars are filled in correctly. The case of *Bramall & Ogden Ltd v. Sheffield City Council* (1983) provides an example of this. The contract was JCT63, with no provision for sectional completion. The Appendix stated that LDs would be 'at the rate of £20 per week for each uncompleted dwelling'. There were 123 dwellings in all. The architect granted certain extensions of time, but the contractor was still late in reaching practical completion. As houses were completed they were taken over by the Council.

The court said that the Council was not entitled to recover LDs because the figure had been stated in terms of each uncompleted dwelling. Since there was no provision for sectional completion, the reduction in LDs once some of the dwellings had been handed back to the Council could be achieved only on the basis of the clause dealing with partial possession. This clause stated that where partial possession was given, the LDs should be reduced proportionally. However, this was not feasible in this case because the LDs figure had not been stated as £20 × 123 (the number of dwellings). There could be no proportionate reduction in '£20 per week for each uncompleted dwelling'. The court was not prepared to allow any adjustment to the wording of the contract to achieve this. It accepted that the argument being raised was very technical, but did not reject it.

Comparison with 'penalties'

The rate of LDs to be inserted into the contract must be a genuine pre-estimate of the loss that the employer will suffer if completion is late. It does not matter if, at a later stage, the sum is no longer accurate. It is sufficient if it was a genuine pre-estimate at the time the contract was made. The test of whether the pre-estimate is genuine is an objective one. In other words the 'genuineness' or honesty of those who arrived at the pre-estimate is not a factor that will be taken into consideration (although their thought processes are likely to be examined).

If the rate of LDs is later disputed by the contractor as being higher than a genuine pre-estimate of loss, the court could say that the clause is void because the sum is a penalty. In that case the employer will usually have an implied right to claim unliquidated damages, and prove their actual loss, but this is likely to be a time-consuming and costly exercise.

If the employer's situation changes after the contract has been entered into, so that the LDs will no longer properly compensate them for delay, the figure cannot be changed unless the contractor agrees. Conversely, if the employer's costs of delay reduce, the contractor will still have to pay the LDs figure in the contract.

It is therefore advisable, for the benefit of all concerned, that the LDs figure in the contract is arrived at after careful consideration and analysis of the likely financial consequences of late completion.

Calculation of LDs

It is useful to keep a record of how the sum has been calculated, in case there is an argument about it later. The calculation will vary depending on the type of project. The case of *Alfred McAlpine v. Tilebox* (2005) provides a useful example of the various factors (set out below) which might be taken into account when determining an appropriate rate of LDs. However, each case will vary depending on its own facts and circumstances. If the employer has engaged a quantity surveyor, they will often assist with the calculation. The figure may include some or all of the following:

- interest incurred during the delay period on interim payments made during construction;
- loss of income from rent;
- cost of alternative accommodation incurred during the delay period;
- extra cost of staging an event in a different venue;
- loss of profit to the business at the property where the works are being carried out;
- any losses which may accrue pursuant to the terms of a development agreement.

If, for some reason, there is no way of accurately calculating the LDs figures on delay, or the figure as calculated is too high to be acceptable to a contractor, the employer has various choices:

- to delete the LDs clause altogether and rely on unliquidated damages if there is delay;
- to agree with the contractor a figure for LDs, and agree that the contractor will not later try to argue that the agreed figure is a penalty;
- to put a figure for LDs into the contract and argue with the contractor later, if necessary, on whether it is a penalty.

Choosing which one of these options to pursue must be the *employer's* decision, not the architect's.

Difficulty in estimating the likely loss is not a reason for the employer to delete the LDs clause altogether, provided, of course, that a figure can be agreed at the time of entering into the contract. There are several cases which support the view that it is precisely in these situations that an LDs clause is most appropriate and effective (see *Clydebank Engineering v. Don Jose Ramos* (1905) and *Dunlop v. New Garage* (1915)). The parties' respective negotiating positions should also be considered where there is any doubt as to the enforceability of the LDs clause. The courts are more likely to uphold the clause if the parties had comparable negotiating strength at the time of entering into the contract.

Local authorities and other publicly funded bodies often make their calculations on a formula basis, by reference to the contract sum at the date of contract. This is not strictly in accordance with judges' views on what is needed for an LDs figure to avoid being a penalty for the private sector, but is likely to be accepted as a valid method of calculation for publicly funded employers, where the factors set out above are not relevant.

The JCT forms

It is essential to follow the procedure for deducting LDs strictly. If the employer fails to do so they may be liable to the contractor for a wrongful deduction of money. The courts are likely to be strict on the employer if they have not followed the procedure correctly and a dispute arises.

It is also essential that a date for completion is fixed and stated in the contract, as well as a sum for LDs inserted.

No loss on late completion?

Even if the employer decides that there will be no loss on a delay to completion, it is dangerous to put '£nil' in the Contract Particulars. This may prevent the employer from claiming *un*liquidated damages if they do later suffer a loss as a result of late completion. It is far better in those circumstances to delete the whole of the liquidated damages clause (*Temloc v. Errill* (1987)).

Procedure for levying LDs

The following table details the elements which are essential in order to operate the procedure under the JCT contracts.

	JCT 1998	**JCT98**	**WCD98**	**IFC98**	**MC98**	**MW98**
(i)	Read the LDs clauses:	24	24	2.6–2.8	2.9–2.11	2.3
(ii)	If the right to LDs arises and there is partial possession read clause:	18.1.4	17.1.4	2.11	2.8	n/a
(iii)	Read the appropriate entry in the Contract Particulars under clause:	24.2	24.2.1	2.7	2.10	n/a
(iv)	Read the clauses on withholding notices:	30.1.1.4 30.8.3	30.3.4 30.6.2	4.2.3(b) 4.6.1.3	4.3.4 4.12.4	4.4.2 4.5.1.3
	JCT 2005	**SBC2005**	**DB2005**	**IC2005**	**MP2005**	**MW2005**
(i)	Read the LDs clause:	2.31 2.32	2.28 2.29	2.22 2.24	16	2.8
(ii)	If the right to LDs arises and there is partial possession, read clause:	2.37	2.34	2.29	17.3	n/a
(iii)	Read the appropriate entry in the Contract Particulars under clause:	2.32.2	2.29.2	2.23.2	16.1	2.8
(iv)	Read the clauses on withholding notices:	4.13.4 4.15.4	4.10.4 4.12.9	4.8.3 4.14.3	29	4.6.2 4.8.3

It is always the employer's decision whether to claim LDs. *The architect's interim and final certificates should not mention LDs*. The terms of the contract should be read in each case but, generally (although the time periods in MP2005 are slightly different), the procedure under most of the JCT forms is as follows:

1. The contractor fails to achieve practical completion by the completion date.
2. The architect issues a non-completion certificate stating that the situation in point 1 has arisen. (If the architect grants an extension of time later it will have the effect of cancelling the non-completion certificate, so another one must be issued if appropriate.)
3. The *employer* tells the contractor in writing before the final certificate is issued that they may require payment of/deduct LDs.
4. Not later than 5 days before the final date for payment of the final certificate either:
   a. the *employer* requires the contractor (in writing) to pay LDs; or

b. the *employer* gives notice in writing of deduction of LDs. (If that notice is not a valid withholding notice the employer must also send the contractor a withholding notice not later than 5 days before the final date for payment of the certificate from which they intend to deduct LDs.)

5. If the architect grants an extension of time after LDs have been paid or deducted, the employer must return the appropriate amount of LDs to the contractor within a reasonable time.

The procedure under MW2005 is somewhat simpler than this, as there is no certificate of non-completion. In addition, MW2005 does not envisage that a further extension of time will be granted after the LDs have been paid, so point 5 of the procedure above would not apply.

In practice, an employer will normally claim LDs long before the final certificate, for various reasons:

- Even in those JCT forms that allow the architect to review extensions of time within 12 weeks of practical completion, this will have been done long before the final certificate is due, so the completion date will be unknown.
- By the time the final certificate is issued, the architect may have already certified (and the employer paid) any further sums due to the contractor, including release of the second half of the retention money.
- The half of the retention money held after practical completion may be insufficient to cover all the LDs.
- It is usually convenient, while the final account is being discussed, to deduct LDs from any further interim certificates issued during that process, if they have not been deducted already.

If the employer intends to deduct LDs from an interim certificate the procedure is similar to that covered in steps 1 to 5 above. The employer must be careful to issue the necessary withholding notices, as otherwise the procedure will be ineffective.

Contractor's delay

LDs can be levied only if the contractor is in delay for reasons that are at the contractor's risk under the construction contract; for example, failure of plant or late delivery of materials for which they are responsible. If the contractor is in delay because of an event that is the responsibility of the employer, or possibly of one of the professional team, the architect must grant an extension of time if the extension of time clause permits.

The architect will normally wish to reach a final conclusion on extensions of time before the employer levies LDs or deducts them from a certificate, because this is more straightforward and less contentious than the employer levying LDs and then returning all or part of them to the contractor when a further extension of time is granted. The benefit of this approach is illustrated by the case of *Reinwood v. Brown* (2007). If it is obvious that the employer will be entitled to deduct LDs, however, even before the architect's final review, there is no reason why the employer should not do so once the contractor is in delay.

See: Timing of award, page 49

Other standard forms

This section has looked at the LDs provisions in the JCT forms (Section 9 looks at the NEC forms). Similar principles apply to LDs clauses in the other standard forms. However, the exact procedure may be different. It is essential to understand and follow those procedures exactly, as the courts adopt a strict interpretation of LDs clauses.

SUMMARY

- Liquidated damages in the JCT forms are the pre-agreed measure of compensation payable for a breach of contract in failing to complete the works by the date for completion. They must be a genuine pre-estimate of the losses likely to be suffered as a result of the delay.
- If the rate of LDs is later disputed by the contractor as being higher than a genuine pre-estimate of loss, the court could rule that the clause is void because the sum is a penalty.
- Where the employer takes partial possession of some of the works before completion, the architect will have to assess what proportion has been taken into possession and, if necessary, apportion LDs accordingly.
- It is vital to follow precisely the procedure for levying LDs laid down in the contract.
- It is useful to keep a record of how the liquidated damages sum has been calculated, in case of later disputes.

Section 3
Grounds for extension of time under the standard forms

In this Section:

- *Acceleration*
- *Delay to completion*
- *Relevant Events*
- *Restrictions on revising the completion date*
- *Minor Works Form*

Introduction

Section 1 explained the reasons for an extension of time clause and some of the basic principles. The JCT forms (apart from MW2005) set out in some detail the procedure for the contractor in relation to delay and extension of time, and it is important for both contractor and architect to follow this procedure closely. If they do not do so, it could be much more difficult to decide what is the proper extension of time to be awarded (if any).

The JCT forms (apart from MW2005 – see page 42) list the *Relevant Events* that can form the grounds for an extension of time. In MP2005 this term is not used, but the concept is similar. The Relevant Events constitute a list of those items that could delay the contractor and for which the employer has taken the risk. One of these is a 'sweep-up' clause, allowing the architect to award an extension of time, for example, for any other act or omission of the employer. This gives the architect a wide scope for awarding extensions. Whichever version of the JCT forms is used, the architect must always check that any extension proposed falls within one of the Relevant Events.

Acceleration

If the contractor is in delay and seeks an extension of time they must also decide whether to accelerate the works at their own cost, either before or after the period allowed to the architect to decide on an extension. If the contractor does so, and the architect subsequently grants an extension, there is no mechanism in the JCT forms to compensate the contractor for the acceleration. Sometimes contractors will ask the employer to agree in advance to pay for acceleration. If the employer does agree, this will be outside the terms of the construction contract and should be administered separately. The employer may, for example, ask the architect to issue certificates in relation to extra payments for acceleration, similar to those under the contract. Payments made for acceleration will similarly be outside the payment regime under the contract (although still governed by the Housing Grants, Construction and Regeneration Act 1996). The architect should be careful not to do anything that could be interpreted as an instruction to accelerate, particularly when communicating with the contractor about the delay.

MP2005 is the only one of the JCT forms that deals with acceleration. The employer can invite proposals from the contractor to achieve practical completion before the completion date, whether the contractor is in delay or not. The contractor should then either make such proposals identifying the time savings and additional costs, or explain why acceleration is impracticable. If proposals are made and agreed, the acceleration will be formally instructed and paid for as part of the contract sum. This is more straightforward than agreeing extra-contractual arrangements with the contractor.

Delay to completion

In considering a notice of delay the architect must decide whether any of the delaying events constitutes a Relevant Event, which will qualify for the grant of an extension, and if so for what period. Before doing so, it is essential to establish whether there has been a delay to completion at all. For instance, it is quite possible for the contractor to experience exceptionally adverse weather conditions, but this may not cause any delay at all if, by that time, the works are weathertight and the external work is not on the critical path. The event identified by the contractor as the cause of delay must be a Relevant Event, and also 'the completion of the Works or of any section [must be] likely to be delayed thereby beyond the relevant Completion Date' (clauses 2.28.1.2 of SBC2005 and 2.25.1.2 of DB2005).

Critical path

This is the sequence of operations through a project network from start to finish, the sum of whose durations determines the overall project duration. See pages 58 and 66 for more detail.

Quite often, particularly on a lengthy and complex project, there will be more than one cause of delay. This is covered in more detail in Section 7. It is important to realise that, for the contractor, some Relevant Events are more attractive than others, because the contractor will use them in order to make a claim for loss and/or expense in addition to an extension of time. If the contractor is successful in this it means that they not only avoid paying LDs for the delay, but are also compensated for the extra time they have had to spend on site because of the delay.

This can sometimes influence the emphasis that the contractor puts on certain causes of delay. For instance, if there is delayed completion caused by exceptionally adverse weather the contractor will be entitled to an extension of time, but this can never be a ground for claiming loss and/or expense. This is therefore a shared risk item between the contractor and the employer. By contrast, if the contractor is delayed because they have received late information from the architect, they will be entitled to an extension of time. They may also be entitled to loss and/or expense. This therefore makes it an attractive ground for an extension of time, for the contractor.

Relevant Events

SBC2005, DB2005 and IC2005 have a very similar list of Relevant Events (clause 2.29 of SBC2005, clause 2.26 of DB2005 and clause 2.20 of IC2005), with the following differences:

- DB2005 includes a ground for 'delay in receipt of any necessary permission or approval of any statutory body which the Contractor has taken all practicable steps to avoid or reduce';
- IC2005 includes a ground relating to named subcontractors.

MP2005 is structured slightly differently and there are some differences in wording. The term 'Relevant Event' is not used. The list of events is more restricted and the following events are not included:

- opening up for inspection where the work, etc. is in accordance with the contract;
- deferring possession of the site (because, under MP2005, the contractor does not gain possession of the site but only access (clause 15.1));
- delay caused by the work carried out by statutory undertakers;
- exceptionally adverse weather conditions;
- civil commotion;
- strikes, lock-outs, etc.

The MW2005 provisions are explained under the heading *Minor Works Form*, page 42. The following paragraphs deal with the Relevant Events listed in SBC2005, DB2005 and IC2005.

Variations and instructions

This Relevant Event is a favourite with contractors because most projects involve a significant number of architect's instructions, for various reasons. These can be variation instructions for instance or, in DB2005, a Change, which is a similar concept. The power to issue instructions arises entirely from the terms of the contract, and there are several clauses that give the architect the power to issue instructions, not always for a variation. Except under MP2005, the contractor has a right to ask under what clause the architect has issued an instruction. Instructions can usually be given orally or in writing, but oral instructions have no effect until confirmed in writing. Under IC2005, there is no power to give instructions orally. Under MP2005 there is no reference to the giving of oral instructions.

Issuing informal instructions

A contractor installed defective piles. In correspondence the contractor put forward alternative proposals to rectify them and asked the architect for an instruction as to which remedial option to adopt. The architect wrote to the contractor saying they should go ahead with one of the alternatives. This was held to be an instruction for a variation, so the contractor was to be compensated for rectifying their own defective work (*Simplex v. London Borough of St Pancras* (1958)).

SBC2005 provides that the architect can decide whether or not to request a 'Schedule 2 quotation' from the contractor. If they decide to follow this route, a quotation is requested, which must be accompanied by sufficient information to enable the contractor to quote. The contractor then supplies a quotation which includes the extension of time required, or alternatively they notify their disagreement with the application of the Schedule 2 quotation procedure being applied (which they must do within 7 days of the notification). Under MP2005, there is a similar, but simplified, procedure.

Late possession of the site

It sometimes happens that the anticipated start date, set out in a letter of intent or the construction contract itself, cannot be met, for example because squatters have occupied the land or because anticipated planning permission has not been given in time. This clause allows the employer to defer possession of the site.

Ideally, the construction contract is executed before work starts on site. Once a date for possession has been inserted into the construction contract, or a binding letter of intent has been issued with a date of possession stated in it, if there is a delay in granting possession, this type of provision will be needed (except under MP2005, where the contractor is not given possession of the site). It is optional and, if it is to be incorporated, the maximum number of weeks for deferring possession (up to 6 weeks) must be stated in the Contract Particulars.

It is important to remember that under the CDM Regulations the employer should not grant possession of the site to the contractor until the construction phase plan is ready. Since this document is rarely ready until just before work is due to start on site, this clause can be useful where for some reason an acceptable construction phase plan has not been produced by the possession date. The JCT forms (apart from MP2005 and MW2005) make this an employer's risk item. The effect of the CDM Regulations is discussed in more detail in Section 1, *When can the works commence?*, page 5.

Without such a clause (or a comprehensive sweep-up clause; see *Any impediment, prevention or default by the employer*, below), if possession is not granted until after the contractual date for possession, the architect has no power to award an extension of time, which means that the delay in granting possession is an act of prevention by the employer, putting time at large, so that the contractor is obliged to complete the works within a 'reasonable time'. This may be different from the contractual completion date.

This is explained in more detail in Section 1, *Does the extension of time clause always apply? Time at large*, page 9.

Suspension for non-payment

The Housing Grants, Construction and Regeneration Act 1996 gives the contractor a right to suspend the works where the employer fails to pay by the final date for payment of an interim or final certificate, having first given at least 7 days' notice of their intention to suspend. Most employers, and their quantity surveyor advisers, are now familiar with the payment regime under the Act. Despite this, there are still cases where the employer wishes to withhold money otherwise due under an interim certificate, but fails to serve a notice of withholding as required by the Act and the JCT forms, not later than 5 days before the final date for payment of that interim amount. The contractor has a right to suspend work and to an automatic extension of time under the Act from the date on which the suspension commenced until the date on which payment is made of the amount withheld. This right exists even if a clause such as this is struck out. Because it is a statutory right, it is not subject to the contractor's general obligation to prevent delay.

Any impediment, prevention or default by the employer

This is a sweep-up clause which covers any act of prevention (or omission) by the employer or those acting for the employer, except to the extent that the contractor or the 'Contractor's Persons' caused or contributed to the delay. This general sweep-up clause will cover any 'impediment, prevention or default' by the employer not covered by any other Relevant Event. In MP2005 the phrase used is 'any other breach or act of prevention' and it will cover late access to the site, which is not covered elsewhere. In deciding whether the contractor caused or contributed to the delay, the architect should check whether there are grounds for an extension of time under any other Relevant Event before considering an award under this Relevant Event. It is a useful clause, as delays do occur from time to time, caused by the employer, which are not covered by any of the other Relevant Events. For instance, the employer may defer possession of the site for more than 6 weeks.

The JCT forms rationalised the list of Relevant Events and made it considerably shorter. Some items that were individually listed in the pre-2005 forms will now fall under this sweep-up clause. These items include those detailed below.

Late information

This is a popular ground with contractors because there is much scope during the course of a construction contract to ask for further information, and for argument over whether it has been provided late or not. SBC2005 and IC2005 provide for an optional Information Release Schedule (IRS) to be produced by the employer at the beginning of the project, setting out the dates by which various items of information will be provided. The employer will usually ask the architect to draw up this document in conjunction with the other consultants, and it is important to put in realistic dates; otherwise it could form the basis for the contractor to claim that they have been delayed by late information.

There is no reason why the contractor should have all the information they will ultimately need, right at the beginning of the project. For instance, ironmongery schedules are not usually required at such an early stage. The dates set out in the IRS should, however, reflect the time taken for delivery of materials that may have a long lead time, and not just the date on which the contractor expects to install them. If the architect is unsure about the lead times for particular materials, they should discuss this with the contractor.

If the architect cannot provide information in accordance with the IRS, for whatever reason, an agreement can be reached with the contractor and the employer that the information will be provided later. This is a somewhat cumbersome procedure, and the employer may not wish to be involved in this type of issue during construction. Rather than relying on this, it is better to spend time putting the correct dates into the IRS at the beginning of the contract.

If, by the time certain information is required, the contractor is in delay and therefore does not yet need it, this does not excuse the architect from providing the information. The dates in the IRS must be met, unless there is agreement otherwise. If the contractor is in delay, however, they may find it difficult to show that late information was the cause of any further delay.

If there is no IRS, the architect is still primarily responsible for providing information at a time when the contractor would reasonably need to have it. If the contractor has reason to believe that the architect is not aware of the time by which they need to receive the further information, they shall, so far as is reasonably practicable, give the architect notice that they need the information. From an architect's point of view this is highly unsatisfactory, because it places the onus on the architect to be aware of what information the contractor needs and when, rather than, as in the wording of earlier JCT contracts, the contractor having the obligation to request information in time for the date when it is needed.

To avoid a claim on this ground, therefore, the architect needs to have as much information as possible listed in the IRS, if there is one. Otherwise, the architect should make regular requests of the contractor, for example at site meetings, for a list of the further information that will be required in the near future, so that it can be provided in time for the contractor. This will not only apply to information such as ironmongery schedules, which rarely need to be provided at the beginning of the project; it also applies to information in the form of clarification of drawings and instructions, where the architect may consider that the contractor already has sufficient information to carry out the construction.

It is also worth remembering the case of *Glenlion Construction v. The Guinness Trust* (1987) (Section 1, page 14): unless the contract states otherwise, the architect is not obliged to provide information to suit the contractor's accelerated programme. SBC2005 and IC2005 expressly apply the *Glenlion* decision.

Although using an IRS as the basis for assessment of delay is more onerous for the architect, it should at least mean that the architect and other designers know in advance when information is required, so that they have time to take instructions from the employer if necessary and prepare the information in accordance with the IRS. The production of the IRS at the beginning of the contract encourages everyone to think ahead about what information will be required, and when.

The assessment of delay arising where there is an IRS is also covered in Section 8, *Provision of information*, page 99.

Workmen engaged direct by the employer

It may be convenient for the employer to have part of the project carried out either by their own in-house staff or by, say, a fit-out contractor. There is often some overlap between the work of the contractor and such people on site. This may be unavoidable, particularly if the employer is working on a fast-track basis.

On some projects the employer also engages the statutory undertakers direct, to carry out work that could form part of the works and which are additional to their statutory powers. This could be convenient for the employer for various reasons. Only delay caused by this extra, non-statutory work is covered under the sweep-up clause.

Where it is known at the beginning of the contract that direct workmen will be engaged, it is sometimes possible to agree with the contractor how far this should be taken into account in drawing up their programme, so as to minimise notifications of delay for this reason.

Free issue materials

Where there are to be free issue materials supplied by the employer, and this causes a critical delay for some reason (for example non-delivery or defective goods) the delay can form a claim under this clause.

CDM Regulations

The operation of the CDM Regulations could delay the works. For instance, the CDM co-ordinator (the successor to the planning supervisor) could raise a safety issue in relation to design carried out by a subcontractor, which could take some time to resolve. Previously this clause allowed for an extension of time where the CDM co-ordinator was carrying out their duties correctly, and even where the employer had failed to ensure that they were doing so (as long as the contractor was not also the CDM co-ordinator). The wording of this clause covered any delay by act or omission of the CDM co-ordinator, which could occur both when the CDM co-ordinator was carrying out the functions and also where there was a failure to do so. It is appropriate to grant extensions under the sweep-up clause if delay is caused for either reason.

Employer's failure to give access

The employer takes the risk of failing to give access to the works if that failure is an 'impediment' by the employer or 'Employer's Persons', which include anyone who is employed or authorised by the employer. In the case of adjacent land or buildings owned by the employer this can give rise to interesting questions: for instance, is the leaseholder of that land authorised by the employer? Arguably, the leaseholder is authorised by the lease to be there, and the contractor is therefore entitled to an extension of time if the leaseholder causes delay by refusing to grant access. For this reason the access to be granted should be set out in one of the contract documents, stating also that if the contractor considers that they may be delayed because of lack of access, they must give reasonable notice, if required, of the need for such access. Sometimes access will be restricted, or given on a phased basis. If so, this should be set out in one of the contract documents. Access can also have health and safety implications. The CDM Regulations require all parties to cooperate with each other and it is in their interests to do so.

Nominated subcontractors or suppliers; named subcontractors

SBC2005 has no provisions for nominated subcontractors or suppliers, unlike the 1998 standard form of JCT contract. IC2005 still retains a provision for named subcontractors. The contractor has a limited responsibility for named subcontractors and IC2005 contains special provisions to deal with the situation where they become insolvent or otherwise cease to carry out any work on the project.

Delay could also be caused by late production of design or installation drawings by named subcontractors. These drawings will usually be subject to comment by a member of the professional team before they can be used for fabrication or construction. If the architect is also the lead designer, they will need to be particularly careful to avoid any delays occurring during this process. It is helpful to specify at the beginning of the project how long the turn-round period will be for drawings, and on larger projects some restriction on the number of drawings which can be submitted at any one time. The contractor does not take responsibility for a delay by a named subcontractor in relation to design or selection of materials. This is one of the reasons why naming is not particularly popular. If a direct agreement between that subcontractor and the employer has been signed, the employer will have the right to sue the named subcontractor for breach of contract if they have delayed the works. This is more cumbersome than making the contractor responsible for all their work.

In the case of named subcontractors the contractor is entitled to an extension of time if delay is caused by the determination of their employment.

Statutory undertakers

This term is defined to include local authorities. Although many of the utilities are now privatised, this does not affect their status as statutory undertakers. If they cause delay to the contractor in carrying out their statutory functions in relation to the works, the contractor will be entitled to an extension of time on this ground. The need for this work should be known at the beginning of the contract, and therefore the contractor should take it into account in drawing up their programme. It is useful to minute this at an early site meeting, if it is not referred to expressly in other contract documents. This could avoid later argument on this point.

Exceptionally adverse weather conditions

This can include not only weather that is cold, wet or windy, but also heatwaves. The clause does not specify how adverse the conditions must be, and the 10-year rule is often applied: that is, the conditions must be more adverse than those that have been experienced in the local area at that time of year over the past 10 years.

The contractor is expected to recognise in their programme that during the winter months there will probably be days when the weather will delay or prevent outside work. However, the contractor may be in delay because of their own fault, which results in a delay, for instance, in making the building weathertight. If exceptionally adverse weather conditions for the time of year then arise during the contract period, the contractor may be entitled to an extension of time. This can happen even though it is the contractor's own delay that has caused the work to be affected by the adverse weather conditions.

> ### *Example*
>
> The contractor was in delay during the course of the contract, according to their programme. Exceptionally adverse weather conditions were then experienced. These conditions further delayed the contractor, because their work was late and more sensitive to bad weather. The court said that the contractor was entitled to an extension of time for the exceptionally adverse weather conditions, even though the contractor might not have been affected by them if they had not already been in delay for reasons that were at their risk (*Walter Lawrence v. Commercial Union* (1984)).

Insured risks

The JCT forms (apart from MW2005) refer to the occurrence of a specified peril as a ground for an extension. This is defined in the JCT forms to include the type of events usually covered by the works insurance.

> ### *Specified perils*
>
> 'Fire, lightning, explosion, storm, flood, escape of water from any water tank, apparatus or pipes, earthquake, aircraft and other aerial devices or articles dropped therefrom, riot and civil commotion, but excluding Excepted Risks' (for example, radioactivity, pressure waves from supersonic aerial devices, etc.) (SBC2005).

Even if, for some reason, the works insurance is not in place, the contractor will be entitled to an extension of time if a delaying event occurs that falls within the definition of specified perils. In making an assessment of the situation, the architect should consider the definition of specified perils, and should ignore the insurance position in deciding whether an extension of time is justified. It does not matter whether the specified peril was caused by the contractor themselves or by one of their subcontractors – for example, a fire on site caused by the unsafe use of hot welding equipment (*Scottish Special Housing Association v. Wimpey* (1986)). This does not apply to MW2005, where on similar wording in an earlier version of the form it has been held that the contractor was liable for a fire caused by their subcontractors' negligence (*The National Trust v. Haden Young* (1994)).

Civil commotion, terrorism etc.

Terrorist activity, or the threat of it, or the actions of public bodies in dealing with it, are all covered by this ground. It can be useful, for example, where there are delays caused by road closures because of a security alert.

Strikes

Strikes, etc. affecting any of the trades employed in the works, or engaged in the manufacture or transportation of goods and materials for the works and which cause delay to the works, would be covered. A strike by employees of a statutory authority would not be covered if their work was not part of 'the Works' (*Boskalis v. Liverpool City Council* (1983)).

Government action

This item was introduced when the Government imposed a 3-day week in the early 1970s. More recently, it has been considered where Government exclusion zones for foot-and-mouth disease affected progress on construction sites.

Force majeure

This phrase has no fixed meaning as far as the UK courts are concerned and the cases are inconsistent regarding its interpretation, possibly because it has been imported from the French Civil Code and does not quite fit with English law concepts. It is often used to mean unforeseen events of catastrophic proportions, sometimes known as acts of God. There are separate clauses in the JCT forms dealing with the effects of a variety of disasters, however, so it is difficult to see in what circumstances this Relevant Event would ever apply.

Unavailability of materials or labour

It is worth noting that unavailability of materials or labour is no longer a ground for an extension of time in the JCT 2005 forms. This clause was almost always deleted, so the omission may not make any difference in most cases.

Restrictions on revising the completion date

Despite being entitled to instruct a variation that is an omission of part of the works, the architect is not entitled to fix a completion date earlier than the date for completion set out in the Contract Particulars. Under clauses 2.25.4 and 2.25.5.2 of DB2005 and 2.28.4 and 2.28.5.2 of SBC2005, if the architect has already awarded an extension of time and then instructs a variation that is an omission, the extension already awarded can be reduced, if appropriate, to take account of the omission. There are two exceptions to this:

- the revised completion date cannot be any earlier than the date for completion as stated in the Contract Particulars; and
- if a revised completion date has been fixed in connection with a 'Pre-agreed Adjustment', that extension of time cannot be reduced unless the relevant change or variation is itself the subject of a Relevant Omission.

Minor Works Form

The extension of time clause in MW2005 (clause 2.2) is completely different in structure from that in the other JCT forms. It provides that the architect is to give any such extension of time 'as may be reasonable' where the works have been or will be delayed beyond the completion date 'for reasons beyond the control of the Contractor'. This includes a variation instruction given by the architect.

The clause states expressly that delay by subcontractors or suppliers, or by the contractor themselves, is deemed to be under the contractor's control. This should mean that where the contractor is responsible for a specified peril, such as a fire on the site, they will not be entitled to an extension of time because this is something under their control. The other JCT forms treat contractor-controlled specified perils differently. There is no provision in MW2005 for any payment of loss and/or expense following the occurrence of events that entitle the contractor to an extension of time. However, in the case of variations the valuation of a variation will include an assessment of other related costs.

See: Relevant events, page 31

SUMMARY

- The Relevant Events constitute a list of those items that could delay the contractor and for which the employer has taken the risk. The architect must always check that any extension proposed falls within one of the Relevant Events.
- If a contractor in delay seeks an extension of time they must also decide whether to accelerate the works at their own cost. However, if the architect subsequently grants an extension, there is no mechanism in the JCT forms to compensate the contractor for the acceleration.
- A notice of delay does not necessarily mean that completion will be delayed if the cause of delay does not affect the critical path.
- As a general rule, the architect may not fix a completion date earlier than that given in the Contract Particulars, even if specifying a variation that omits part of the works.
- The extension of time clause in MW2005 has a different structure to the other JCT forms insofar as it does not contain a list of Relevant Events and instead requires the architect to give a reasonable extension where the works have been delayed beyond completion 'for reasons beyond the control of the Contractor'.

Section 4
Notification of delay

In this Section:

- *Giving notice of delay*
- *Timing and contents of notice*
- *Methods of notification*
- *Supporting information*
- *Timing of award*

Giving notice of delay

The contractor must give notice to the architect that there is delay to the works. This notice must be given to the architect, except under DB2005, where it is to be given to the employer's agent unless the employer has stated that it is to be given to the employer directly. Under MP2005 the notice must be given to the employer's representative.

Contractor's programme shows early completion

If the contractor's programme shows that they are intending to finish the works before the date for completion and a delay occurs, the contractor should still give notice of delay even if it will not push the completion date beyond the contractual date for completion. If a delay occurs in these circumstances and the architect believes that the contractor will still complete by the date for completion in the contract, the architect is not obliged to grant any extension of time (see *Who owns the float on the contractor's programme?*, page 56).

All the JCT forms require the contractor to give notice of delay, and this should be in writing. The contractor's notice triggers the operation of the extension of time clause. The architect has no power to grant an extension of time during the course of the construction works unless such a notice has been given.

Occasionally a contractor will not give notice of delay where they have been delayed either by matters that are at their own risk or by those that are at the employer's risk but which do not also form the basis for a claim for loss and/or expense (such as exceptionally adverse weather). This may be because the contractor is hoping that some other event will arise, such as the instruction of a variation, which will enable them to claim both an extension of time and loss and/or expense, and they do not wish to highlight these other delaying factors. If the architect believes this is happening, the delaying event can be recorded in the minutes of site meetings. This will then be a useful record for the future, particularly in relation to concurrency of delay: see Section 7.

Technically, a failure by the contractor to give notice of all delays is a breach of contract. The architect can take this into account in assessing an extension of time. In an extreme case, the architect may decide that the contractor is not entitled to the extension they seek because part of the delay is attributable to the contractor's own delays, or could even have been avoided if the contractor had given earlier notice of delays for reasons that are at the employer's risk.

Contractor in increasing delay

If the architect considers that the contractor is in delay because of their own default, and that the delay is increasing, this can be a sign of the contractor falling into financial difficulties and being unable to pay their subcontractors to continue working on site. Alternatively, it could mean that the contractor has management difficulties. It is important for all parties to face up to these issues and not let the contract drift further into delay.

The consequences of failing to give adequate notice of delay have been explored in decisions both in England and other Commonwealth jurisdictions. In *Gaymark v. Walter Construction* (1999), the Australian courts said that a failure by the contractor to comply with a strict contractual requirement to give notice of delay meant that the extension of time mechanism was not activated. The project having gone into delay (part of which was the employer's responsibility), the court held that time was at large and the employer lost their entitlement to LDs.

On the other hand, the English courts took a different view in the subsequent case of *Multiplex v. Honeywell* (2007) and stated that where it is possible for the contractor to comply with the notice requirements, but they simply fail to do so, this will not set time at large. The court suggested that to adopt the *Gaymark* approach in such cases would allow the contractor to disregard the provisions regarding the giving of proper notice of delay and thereby set time at large at their own election.

If the contractor does not give notice when they are in delay, under most of the forms (except MW2005) the architect can still grant extensions in the 12 weeks after practical completion, if sufficient justification exists. In MP2005 this is subject to the contractor providing more information to support a claim for an extension of time.

See: Timing of award, page 49

Timing of notice

The JCT forms require the contractor to give notice when 'it becomes reasonably apparent that the progress of the works is being or is likely to be delayed'. MW2005 is worded slightly differently, but the effect is the same. The notice is to be given forthwith. There are good reasons for this: if notice is given as soon as a delay is identified, it may be possible for the delay to be reduced or avoided, either by the contractor using their best endeavours, which they are contractually required to do, or by the relevant member of the professional team making some adjustment to the design. On a large project, where delay can have major implications, it may be worth, say, the architect agreeing to the use of a different type of material that is more readily available than the one originally specified, if non-availability of a material is causing delay.

See: Best endeavours, page 80

Contents of notice

The notice of delay should not only be in writing, and given to the correct person, it should also contain the information required by the contract. In the case of SBC2005 and DB2005 the contractor must state:

• the material circumstances;
• the cause or causes of the delay;
• any event that the contractor considers is a Relevant Event.

Either with the notice or as soon as possible afterwards, the contractor must provide in writing:

- particulars of the expected effects of the factors identified in the notice; and
- an estimate of the extent of the expected delay, whether or not it is concurrent with any other delay.

The contractor is also required to give any further notices needed to keep the particulars and estimate of delay up to date, and provide further information on request.

MP2005 and IC2005 do not go into such detail: the contractor is required merely to give notice of the cause of the delay. Under these forms, therefore, the contractor is not required to identify the extent of the delay or to give any further notices to the architect to keep the information up to date.

IC2005: further information

IC2005 states that the contractor shall provide such information required by the architect as is reasonably necessary for the purpose of making an assessment of an extension of time. The contractor can therefore wait for the architect to ask for more information. The architect should identify, soon after receiving the notice, what further information is required, and ask the contractor for it, in writing.

MW2005, as expected, is far simpler, and merely requires that the contractor shall notify the architect if it is apparent that the works will not be completed by the date for completion, and the architect must then make a reasonable extension of time. The contractor is not required to provide any details in their notice, or to assess the extent of the delay. There is no time within which the architect should grant an extension under MW2005, although logically this should be before practical completion is achieved.

Methods of notification

It is in the contractor's interest to give notice of delay with all the relevant background information to enable the architect to award an extension of time, but during the course of construction this is often not done. Sometimes the contractor will try to argue that the dates in their programme constitute notice of the dates on which information is required. This is relevant to a pre-1998 version of JCT80, and is based on the old case of *London Borough of Merton v. Stanley Hugh Leach Ltd* (1985). That was a dispute about the JCT1963 contract, in which the extension of time clause was significantly different from those in the JCT forms. In the modern forms a notice of delay must be specific to the particular delay in question, and any document prepared for the contract months in advance, for another purpose, is unlikely to be satisfactory as a notice of delay at a later stage. If there is a difference of opinion with a contractor about an application for extension of time, it is *essential* to consult the exact wording of the contract. The contractor must comply with the notice clause in the contract, and general principles set out in cases decided by the court do not apply if they are inconsistent with the wording of the contract itself.

Sometimes a contractor will use a standard letter in notifying delay, and this can be acceptable as long as it contains all the information required by the contract, as set out above. It is unlikely, therefore, that a standard letter that is used in exactly the same form throughout the course of a contract will be satisfactory, as circumstances will differ. An architect faced with such a letter should not delay in requesting whatever further information is required in order to make an assessment of the delay notified.

Supporting information

It is in the interests of all parties that supporting information is provided as soon as possible after a delay has been identified, because it is very much easier to make an accurate assessment of delay when the events are fresh in everyone's minds, rather than waiting until later when subsequent events could have clouded the issue. Although not all forms specifically provide for the architect to request more information, if it is needed it is best to ask for it, soon after receiving the notice.

Timing of award

Having received the notice and (except under MW2005) the particulars of the expected effects, the architect must make an award as soon is reasonably practicable, and in any event within a period of 12 weeks (6 weeks under MP2005). Under SBC2005 and DB2005 this period does not start until those particulars have been received by the architect. Where notice of delay is given less than 12 weeks before the completion date, the architect should endeavour to make the award no later than the completion date.

Partial information received

The architect can grant an extension based on the information received and, if the contractor subsequently provides more information, this may assist the architect in the review of extensions after practical completion.

The architect may decide that, having received the particulars and estimate from the contractor, it is not fair and reasonable to fix a later date. If that is the architect's view, the contractor must be notified as soon as reasonably practicable or at the latest by the end of the 12-week period. There may be circumstances where the architect does not think it is appropriate to award an extension of time, for instance if no extension is justified, or if the information provided is incomplete.

It is sensible to consider the timing of any award of an extension of time in the context of the contract as a whole. In *Reinwood Ltd v. L Brown & Sons Ltd* (2008) a certificate of non-completion was issued only a few weeks before the award of an extension of time. In the intervening period an interim certificate was issued. The employer, Reinwood, relied on the notice of non-completion, and served a notice of intention to withhold payment in respect of liquidated damages. Reinwood then paid the balance due under the interim certificate, 4 days before the final date for payment. Brown argued that the subsequent extension of time had the effect of invalidating the notice of non-completion, and the notice of intention to withhold payment on which it was based. On appeal, the court said that the notice of intention to withhold payment was not invalidated by the subsequent award of an extension of time. That decision was recently upheld by the House of Lords.

It is not good practice for the architect to delay awarding an extension of time simply on the grounds of wanting to see what kind of progress the contractor can make, and how far the contractor will be able to reduce or avoid delay. Architects used to do this under earlier versions of the JCT forms, but it should not be necessary now, particularly because most of the forms allow the architect a further 12 weeks after practical completion to reassess the extensions of time awarded, and to make adjustments if appropriate.

Theoretically, the architect could make this review before practical completion, but since the wording of the JCT forms which contain this provision allows for only one reassessment, it is better to leave this until after practical completion in most circumstances. The 12-week period after practical completion appears to be mandatory, but in *Temloc v. Errill* (1987) the court said that 'it is directory only as to time'. It is not good practice, however, to take more than 12 weeks in carrying out the final review of extensions.

Review of extensions

The JCT forms (apart from MW2005) provide that the architect shall review the extensions granted (and refused) and award an extension or further extensions if considered appropriate, in the 12 weeks after practical completion. On that review the architect can reduce extensions already granted, except (in the case of SBC2005 and DB2005) an extension of time agreed as part of a 'Pre-agreed Adjustment' for a variation or change (see *Restrictions on revising the completion date*, page 42). In IC2005 this review is optional and in MP2005 the review is dependent on the provision by the contractor of documentation to support any further adjustment to the completion date.

SUMMARY

- The JCT forms require the contractor to give notice to (in most cases) the architect that there is delay to the works.
- An architect who believes that the contractor is in delay, where the contractor has failed to give a notice of delay, should make a record of this in the minutes of the site meetings.
- The timing of the notice is vital. The JCT forms require the contractor to give notice when 'it becomes reasonably apparent that the progress of the works is being or is likely to be delayed'.
- The notice of delay must detail the material circumstances, the cause of the delay and state any event that the contractor considers is a Relevant Event.
- Supporting information should be provided as soon as possible after a delay has been identified, while the events are still fresh in everyone's minds.
- Having received the notice of delay and reports of expected effects on the completion date, the architect must make an award as soon as reasonably practicable, and in any event within a period of 12 weeks.
- In the 12 weeks after practical completion the architect will also have an opportunity to review previous extensions and award any further extensions considered appropriate.

Section 5
Supply of information

In this Section:

- *Contractor's responsibility*
- *Where the architect already has information*
- *Time limits*
- *Form of submission*
- *If no information or insufficient information is provided*
- *Who owns the float on the contractor's programme?*
- *Form of programme*
- *As-built and intended programmes*

Contractor's responsibility

Section 4 sets out the basic requirements of the notice of delay that the contractor is required to provide to the architect.

The contract may also require the contractor to supply other information that would assist the architect in considering extensions of time, such as a programme, which is to be updated at regular intervals. Section 4 also sets out some of the information that the contract may require the contractor to supply.

If the notice of delay is not clear to the architect it would be reasonable for the architect to ask for clarification. It would not be reasonable for the architect to request a 'claim' from the contractor. A 'claim' would be a document from the contractor setting out all the detail of the event or events that the contractor maintained were causing a delay to completion, including the notice or notices, supporting correspondence, diagrams and programmes. The contractor may *choose* to submit such a document, but the architect should never request the contractor to submit one.

If the contractor has supplied an adequate notice and any other information that the contract requires, the responsibility to provide information to the architect has been discharged.

Where the architect already has information

On receiving a notice of delay, the architect may believe that all the information necessary to assess the claim has already been provided, or the architect may simply have a good 'feel' for the causes of delay to the contractor. It is still a good idea, except in the simplest of cases, to ask the contractor whether they have any further information to support their notice. There may be documents of which the architect is unaware, or other factors that are not obvious and that have not previously been brought to the architect's attention. For instance, the cause of the delay to completion may be some event that the architect does not know about. It is only by obtaining full information about what was happening at the time of the delay that the architect can make a proper assessment.

Example

- The construction of the Malmaison Hotel in Manchester was completed late and the architect granted an extension of time, but not for the full period of delay.
- The contractor notified a delay and subsequently claimed an extension of time in arbitration proceedings, because of variations and late information.
- The employer argued that the contractor's reasons for claiming an extension of time were not valid because those events were not on the critical path.
- The employer also alleged that the true causes of the delay were other matters that were not Relevant Events, and for which the contractor was responsible.

Following the determination of certain issues by the arbitrator, the case came to court. The judge said that the employer was entitled to raise these other matters as a defence to the claim for an extension of time, as well as saying that the contractor's reasons were not on the critical path. The contractor was basing his assessment of delay on a revised programme that allegedly ignored the true state of the works (*Henry Boot v. Malmaison* (1999)).

Time limits

Except under MP2005, which states that the contractor must provide documentation in support of any further extension of time no later than 42 days after practical completion, there are no express time limits within which information is to be provided. Under SBC2005 and DB2005 the 12-week period for the architect to make an assessment of extensions of time does not begin to run until the particulars of the expected effects of the delaying event have been received, except where the notice of delay is given within 12 weeks of the completion date. It is in the interest of both architect and contractor that any further information required be requested as soon as possible after the notice of delay has been received. The information should be provided speedily by the contractor. This will enable the 12-week period to start running under SBC2005 and DB2005.

For all the JCT forms it is sensible to request the information and to set a reasonable time limit for its production. At the end of that period the architect can then make a further request for that information, if it has not been provided, which should allow for better management of the extension of time request than giving the contractor no indication of when the information is expected.

If the information is not received by the end of the contractual time period for awarding an extension of time, the architect must, of course, make an award on the basis of information that is available: see *If no information or insufficient information is provided*, page 56.

The judge in *The Royal Brompton Hospital NHS Trust v. FA Hammond and Ors* (2000) said that the architect's conduct in making an award of an extension of time 'has to be judged having regard to the information available to him, or which ought to have been available to him, at the time he gave his advice or made his decision or did whatever else it is that he did'.

Form of submission

The JCT forms do not specify in detail the form in which the information is to be provided, and therefore it is for the architect to specify whether the information should be provided in a particular way, for example as an amended programme, or by providing written details that substantiate the causes of the delay and its extent. The more specific the architect can be, the more likely it is that the information provided will be what is needed. It is best, however, to state at the same time that the contractor is free to supply whatever further information they consider is necessary in support of their notification.

If no information or insufficient information is provided

If the contractor does not supply the information required, or the information they do supply is insufficient, this does not relieve the architect from the duty to make the best use of the information available.

Even with a complete lack of information from the contractor, the architect would be expected to have some knowledge and understanding of the progress of the works and the impact on progress of events for which the architect was responsible, such as instructions and release of information.

If the contractor does not supply the information required, in practical terms their problem will be that the architect is likely to be conservative in assessing the event. This would not be unreasonable under the circumstances.

Who owns the float on the contractor's programme?

- *Float* is defined as the time available for an operation in addition to its planned duration.
- *Free float* is the time by which an operation may be delayed or extended without affecting the start of any succeeding operation.
- *Total float* is the time by which an operation may be delayed or extended without affecting the contract duration.

The ownership of the float on the contractor's programme is an issue that is much debated. At the simplest level it can be argued that the terms of the contract answer the question. For an extension of time to be awarded there must be a delay to completion.

Example

A single operation contract has a completion period of 10 weeks, and the contractor shows 1 week of float at the end of the period. At week 5 the architect issues an instruction for further work, which takes the whole of week 6 to execute. According to the contractor's progress at week 5, they were due to complete at the end of week 9, or one week early: therefore there would be no delay to completion as a result of the additional work as the contract would still complete by week 10 (see Figure 5.1).

FIGURE 5.1: *Instructions for further work: impact on completion period*

	1	2	3	4	5	6	7	8	9	10
Contract period										
Anticipated completion at week 5										
Instruction at week 6										

▦ Period during which the further work was carried out

The contractor completes at week 10, so there is no delay to the contract.

It would not be relevant whether or not the contractor declares the float if a proper analysis of progress is being undertaken.

Alternatively, if the contractor had suffered a delay that was at their own risk – that is, one that would not give rise to an extension of time – at week 4, then by the same analysis at week 5 progress would show that completion would be at week 10 and therefore the additional work would cause a delay to completion of 1 week (see Figure 5.2).

FIGURE 5.2: *Earlier delay and instructions for further work: impact on completion period*

	1	2	3	4	5	6	7	8	9	10	11
Contract period											
Anticipated completion at week 5											
Instruction at week 6											

▥ Period of contractor's delay at their own risk

▦ Period during which the further work was carried out

So, at the simplest level neither the employer nor the contractor owns the float. The contract owns the float, in the sense that it can be used to cover any event that occurs which puts the completion date at risk.

Form of programme

Minimum requirements

The contract should set out the minimum requirements that should be shown on the programme. The complexity and nature of the project will affect the amount of detail to be shown on the programme. The programme should usually be in bar chart format (Gantt chart) and prepared using *critical path network methodology.*

Critical path network methodology is the process of deducing the critical activities or tasks in a programme by tracing logical sequences of activities or tasks that directly affect the completion date. Critical path activities are those that must reach the stages shown on the chart before the next critical path activity can start. Other activities may go on around the critical activities.

Ideally, as a minimum, the programme should show the following:

- all activities (there should be some restriction on the length of any activity before it is broken down into sub-activities) showing earliest and latest start and finish dates;
- the critical path or paths;
- milestones and key dates;
- holiday periods;
- submission and approval dates and periods for the contractor's design work (if applicable);
- submission and approval dates and periods for samples to be provided by the contractor;
- procurement periods for major items of work or specialist items which are difficult to obtain;
- dates of any tests by the employer;
- dates for information to be supplied by the architect or employer;
- commissioning periods;
- float;
- resources;
- any restraints given in the contract, such as sectional completion, phasing or access dates.

In an ideal world all programmes would be generated by computer software.

Programme scheduling software

It is not proposed to go into the finer points and merits, or otherwise, of the respective packages that are available. Each package has its promoters and detractors. Some might argue that it is a matter of taste, familiarity and – for larger contractors – the needs of the company. However, some general comments can be made:

- *Microsoft Project:* This is probably the most commonly used software available. It is relatively inexpensive but powerful. The added advantage is that most organisations have a copy somewhere and can therefore read and manipulate the data. It generally transfers between updates and is relatively easy to use at an elementary level due to Microsoft 'layout' and standard tools. The graphics are fairly basic.
- *Primavera*: This is generally considered to be the most advanced and expensive application. It has excellent trademark graphics and tools. It generally requires operator training in order to get the most out of it and is strictly licensed. There are also several variations (e.g. Suretrak) and enhancements (e.g. Pertmaster) which complement the package and make it a common choice of professional planners. It is possible to import Microsoft Project data into the Primavera programmes.
- *Asta Powerproject*: This is a good quality, medium priced package. It is much favoured by contracting organisations in the UK. The graphics can be manipulated but it is not as sophisticated as Primavera. It is strictly licensed.

Online project hosting and data handling systems and organisations

A number of online project hosting and data handling systems have evolved over the past few years, sometimes known as 'extranets'. There is competition between these systems and they do not all survive long enough to become established providers. Essentially they are a data storage and retrieval system for individual projects, the aim being to reduce multiple storage, printing and data handling. All parties store the data on a secure website, which is accessed by password. This is a source of 'total' information and should provide a complete documentary history of the project. There are a great number of these sites, for instance:

- Primavera: www.primavera.com
- Aconex: www.aconex.co.uk

Non-standard or bespoke packages should be avoided, for at least two reasons. First, training would be required to make any user familiar and efficient with the programme, and the programme package is unlikely to represent value for money for a potentially one-off situation. Readers or interpreters of the programme will need to be trained accordingly.

Second, if computer software is to be used on a project, the contract should state the package to be used. There is no point in the architect using a different package from the contractor. It is feasible, but would require either the architect (the more likely option) or the contractor to re-create the programme in their own software package. This would be a waste of resources, and might not exactly replicate the logic of the original programme.

The contract should also provide for the project programme to be transferred electronically from one party to the other.

As-built and intended programmes

As-built programme

Ideally, the as-built programme should be agreed between the contractor and the architect as the work proceeds. If it cannot be agreed, the architect should maintain a separate as-built programme. It is expensive in time and resources to create an as-built programme after completion, even when there are good records. On very small contracts it is probably unrealistic to consider producing an as-built programme, but the architect should be aware of the start and completion of the major operations even on a small contract.

The as-built programme should, ideally, be based on the original programme operations and should show, as a minimum, the start and end date of all the operations.

The as-built programme need not show any logic links or critical path; it is a record of actual progress of activities.

Intended programmes

Intended programmes are the subsequent updates of the original programme showing progress to date (ideally), planned progress to completion and the anticipated completion date or dates.

The intended programmes should follow the same format as the original programme. New operations should not be introduced unless they are entirely new (that is, they are introduced as a result of a variation), or they are a subset of an existing operation, in which case it should be clearly identified that this is the case.

The contract should state how frequently intended programmes should be issued.

SUMMARY

- In addition to the notice of delay, the contract may also require the contractor to supply other information that would assist the architect in considering extensions of time.
- The architect should obtain as much information as possible from the contractor to assist in assessing the requirement for an extension of time.
- Only MP2005 sets a time limit within which the contractor must provide documentation in support of any further extension of time. However, it is advisable for the architect to give the contractor a set time within which to produce the information.
- The project owns the float unless the contract states otherwise.
- The architect and contractor should preferably use the same programming software.

Section 6
Assessing an extension of time

In this Section:

- *Time limits*
- *Analysing information*
- *The calendar period; the working day/week*
- *The working cycle; working week and the seasons*
- *Individual activity delays*
- *Variations: additional work; late variations*
- *Best endeavours*
- *Making an interim award*
- *No programme*
- *Further assessment after practical completion*

Time limits

SBC2005 and DB2005 give the architect 12 weeks to make a decision on an extension of time. Where the contractor gives a notice of delay less than 12 weeks before practical completion, the architect must endeavour to make the decision by practical completion. In all other cases, the 12-week period starts when the contractor has given the architect notice of the delay and its expected effects, including an estimate of the delay to completion. See Section 4 for the basic requirements of the notice.

Analysing information

It is important to have as full a picture as possible of the reasons for delay, and there are a number of sources of information that the architect can find useful when considering delays to a contract:

- the notice of delay;
- site progress meetings;
- contractor's reports;
- construction programme;
- method statements;
- daywork sheets and contractor's allocation sheets;
- clerk of works' reports and diaries;
- other members of the professional team;
- as-built construction programme; and
- observation.

Notice of delay

Most forms of contract state the basic requirements of the notice of delay. Generally, the usual minimum notification requirement is to state the cause and the period or estimated period of the delay.

The notice requirements in the JCT forms are dealt with in Section 4.

If all other sources of information are absent and no monitoring is taking place, such as the compilation of an as-built programme, the notice of delay may be the only indication of a delay that the architect receives, and the only information on which a decision can be based.

If the notice is the only information the architect has or can obtain, it is a question of the architect making the best use of the information given in the notice. Ultimately, except where the contract states otherwise, lack of information is not a reason for failing to make an assessment of delay.

Site progress meetings

Site progress meetings are usually concerned with progress in the broadest sense: that is, how the works are proceeding so as to achieve the date for completion, and any action to be taken by the architect so that the contractor is not prevented from achieving that date.

The meeting should therefore review the provision of information to the contractor, the effect of variations and the causes of delay, and how these can, if possible, be overcome or mitigated.

The question of whether the architect has received a valid notice of delay as a result of site meeting minutes has been discussed in Section 4.

The architect may be told in the meeting about the cause or causes of delay to the completion of the contract, which will need to be weighed against the documented evidence of delay or personal observation. It is crucial that, wherever possible, the architect compares evidence of progress or delay from various sources, as there can often be inconsistent reports, which need to be cross-checked.

Contractor's reports

The contractor often provides a report to the architect for discussion at the site progress meeting, which is then usually appended to the site meeting minutes. The contract may require the contractor to notify all delays, and they often do this through the medium of their report.

A contractor's report may state that the contract will not reach practical completion until 2 weeks after the date for completion because of a particular Relevant Event. Subsequently, at a later date, the contractor may argue that the delay was 4 weeks for that Relevant Event.

What the contractor states the delay to be, although it may be relevant to their contractual obligations of notification, may not in fact be at all relevant to the actual delay. The architect may believe the extent of the delay to be something different, such as 1 week. In the final analysis it will be a matter of fact, albeit based on some assessment, as to what the delay to completion is or was.

Where the architect may be considering the contractor's subsequent opinion of the period of delay, the contemporaneous evidence – that is, the contractor's reports – could be significant if, in the knowledge of the contractor's reported delay, the architect made decisions in order to mitigate the delay, which then had an impact on subsequent operations.

Construction programme (activity/time schedule)

An architect should have at least a rudimentary understanding of the principles of construction programming.

The detail in any construction programme varies from contract to contract, and usually depends on the complexity of the works, but there are some fundamental principles that apply to any construction programme. One is that it should show

how the contractor proposes to execute the works. It is both the contractor's responsibility as to how they proceed and their right, in the absence of anything to the contrary in the contract documents, to complete the contract in any manner they see fit. It is therefore arguable that the construction programme need not be entirely accurate, or even show the sequence in which the work is actually carried out.

Under the JCT forms the contractor's programme is not a contract document; therefore it is not binding on the parties.

If the parties are tempted to make the contractor's programme a contract document (which is not recommended), they should remember that the contractor's programme is, in reality, a document that is subject to change of varying degrees.

However refined the contractor's planning methods are, the construction programme is still only a subjective assessment based on experience and judgment of how the works can be carried out. Within the construction programme the period shown for each individual operation is only an indication of how long it is likely to take and how it interacts with other operations. It is therefore, to a certain extent, notional.

The construction programme should be regarded as a flexible management tool, and not something that is cast in stone as immutable fact.

The programme ought to show a *critical path*; that is, the sequence of operations that, if delayed, will have a delaying effect on the completion date of the contract. There may be one critical path or there may be more than one. Where there is more than one they may be interrelated. The programme should also show links between operations, lead and lag times, and when the contractor requires information.

However, on some contracts, especially small projects, the programme may show none of this information. The programme may simply be a bar chart giving the duration and sequence of each operation.

Although the construction programme is the contractor's management tool, showing how they intend to progress the works, it is also a useful tool for the architect. It enables the architect to:

- monitor the contractor's progress, to identify delay and to monitor information requirements so as to prevent delay;

- be aware when instructions and information need to be issued so as not to be the cause of a delay;
- assess extensions of time.

Progress should be monitored against the current intended programme.

Financial programme

The architect may find it of value, particularly on larger projects, to request details of the contractor's cash-flow forecast showing the estimated gross valuation of the works at the date of each monthly certificate over the duration of the contract. This information can then be used to draw a graph of the anticipated spend against which the architect can record the actual spend taken from the monthly certificates. If the actual spend drops behind the cash-flow forecast this is a useful indicator of how much the contractor needs to increase the monthly spend to get back on programme because 'spend' usually reflects the level of activity on site and less spend means less activity. This information can then be used to see whether the reported delays in the construction programme, if any, correspond with what the financial programme is indicating.

The cash-flow forecast for a typical project will follow what is known as a 'lazy S' curve (a forward slanting S shape). The architect could prepare an estimated cash-flow forecast for their own use if the information was not forthcoming from the contractor, showing time on the x axis and spend on the y axis. A clause requiring this information is often added to the Preliminaries.

Method statements

These are written to show that the contractor understands the work and has thought it though and planned it properly and safely. The sequencing of the individual parts of a task will affect how the planner puts the programme together, and this is why the method statement should be cross-referenced to the activities on the programme. Sometimes the contractor submits a method statement with the construction programme. Some activities within the construction programme, such as demolition or piling, can have individual method statements.

Comments similar to those about construction programmes can be made about method statements. However, it can be argued that method statements provide an even more rigid framework within which to operate than a construction programme, since they provide a more detailed statement of the sequence and interrelationship of activities.

Because the information in the method statement is so detailed, if the contractor deviates from it and a delay occurs there will be an inference that the deviation has caused or contributed to the delay, whether or not any action of the contractor has influenced the delay.

Daywork sheets and contractor's allocation sheets

Daywork sheets, whether they have been used to value a variation or the contractor has presented them for 'record purposes', are an excellent means, if verified, of establishing when work was executed. However, these are only used to record work where no other method of valuation exists. Contractor's allocation sheets, if the contractor makes them available to the architect, can also be useful, but they are the contractor's own records and must provide sufficient verifiable detail of work executed before they can be relied on.

Clerk of works' reports and diaries

Although traditional clerks of works are less common now, the function of observation and recording of information is still undertaken, normally by visiting consultants such as project managers, architects, engineers and quantity surveyors, and this should be encouraged. Clerks of works or these consultants often provide reports giving their version of delays and matters affecting progress, which may or may not accord with those presented by the contractor. Either the clerk of works, another member of the professional team or the contractor may take regular progress photographs and these can be a useful factual record.

If the clerk of works and the contractor both perceive a delay then it is very likely that there *is* a delay, even though its cause and duration may be a matter of disagreement and the contractor may not have given any formal notification.

The clerk of works may also keep a diary, which can provide a useful source of information on day-to-day events.

Other members of the professional team

It is perfectly acceptable for the architect to seek the views and opinions of other members of the design team, and they will often have useful information, particularly about progress on the work they have designed. However, the extension of time award should be seen as the architect's independent opinion.

As-built construction programme

Arguably the most vital source of information in monitoring progress and assessing delay is a document that records when:

- operations actually began and finished;
- variations were issued and executed;
- information was released and the work involved was executed.

Unless there is a clear picture of how the works are actually being executed it is very difficult to make any logical decision concerning progress or causes of delay.

An as-built programme should be compiled as the works proceed, and should be agreed by the architect and the contractor as a record of fact.

Unfortunately, it is often the case that the as-built programme has to be put together by both parties after completion to establish with any certainty what actually happened. By then, as a result of poor and contradictory records of the progress of the works, it is difficult to establish with any certainty when an activity actually began and ended.

It is essential to compile the as-built programme as the works progress, while the information is fresh in everyone's minds. Modern programming software can provide a base line for the project and record actual progress as the works are carried out.

Observation

A prerequisite of observation is an understanding of the construction process and experience of assessing the rate of progress by watching construction operations. The architect may find it useful to look at the overall number of workers on site and whether all available areas are being worked on. If there are people standing around idle, this could be as a result of poor management or because the contractor has failed to arrange for the necessary materials to be available when needed, or has failed to sequence the works efficiently. It could also, of course, be the result of lack of design information or bad weather.

Watching the construction progress on the site in comparison with the programme, if there is one, can assist the architect in forming a view on whether the works will be completed by the contract completion date.

The calendar period

There is always the temptation to make the award in 'working days' and then convert the award to calendar days. This temptation should be resisted. The contract is to be performed in a calendar period, starting on one date and finishing on another, therefore any awards of an extension of time should be made on the same calendar basis.

The standard forms of contract do not provide for an extension of time for trade or public holidays or, for that matter, for weekends as such. These calendar events have to be considered in relation to the period of delay into which they fall (see Figure 6.2).

The working day/week

The duration of the working day may vary from season to season. There may also be restrictions on the duration of the working week. For the purpose of the examples given in this section, a 5.5 day working week has been assumed.

If the employer wishes to restrict the working day or working week, this must, of course, be stated in the contract. There may also be statutory or local authority restrictions on the working day or week, which also need to be stated in the contract.

Apart from the seasons themselves, the environment within which the works are executed may also restrict the working day or week.

All of these potential restrictions need to be understood by the architect. The responsibility for accommodating these restrictions in the contract period may be that of the contractor or the employer, and the architect needs to look at the contract documents to know which is the responsible party.

The contractor should always be asked to state the working hours on which their tender was based, although they are deemed to have allowed for the effect of weekends and holidays within the original contract period. They are also deemed to have allowed for the effect of the seasons within the original contract period, except in the case, for example, of SBC2005, DB2005 and IC2005, where they are relieved of the risk of exceptionally adverse weather.

The working cycle

The effect of the cycle of a particular operation on the effective working day can be illustrated by an example: see Figure 6.1.

FIGURE 6.1: *Impact of delays on working cycle*

Hours (working day)	1	2	3	4	5	6	7	8	9	10
Planned first pile										
Planned second pile										
Delay event										
Actual piles completed (1 No.)										

Period of delay

A bored pile operation is to be undertaken, and the piling rig can complete two piles per day. Owing to the nature of the operation, a pile must be completed within its cycle: once the hole is bored, the reinforcement must be placed and the concrete poured. The pile must not be left open. If an event occurs that causes a delay of 2 hours, this will affect the piling cycle and will prevent a pile from being completed within the cycle. Therefore half a working day is lost as a result of the delay event, not just 2 hours. This can be an important consideration when there is a restriction on working outside normal working hours.

Working week and the seasons

The effect of the length of the working week on an operation or activity can also be illustrated by an example. Figure 6.2 shows a delay where the delaying event begins on a Monday.

The contractor's working week is Monday to Friday and half-day Saturday. The working days lost by the delay are 5, and this also represents 5 calendar days. Figure 6.3 shows the same delay, but on this occasion the delaying event begins on a Thursday. Five working days are lost, but this translates into 6.5 calendar days.

FIGURE 6.2: *Impact of a delay occurring at the beginning of the working week*

Days		M	T	W	T	F	S	S	M	T	W	T
Working week												
Delay event												
Period of delay												

FIGURE 6.3: *Impact of a delay occurring mid-week*

Days		M	T	W	T	F	S	S	M	T	W	T
Working week												
Delay event												
Period of delay												

The same principle applies in considering the effect of trade holidays falling within the period of delay. Figure 6.4 illustrates the position where an operation programmed for 13 calendar days takes 26.5 days to complete as a result of a delaying event. The direct effect of the delay is only 5 working and 5 calendar days, but there is a consequential effect of 8.5 calendar days because of a trade holiday and a weekend.

The contractor is deemed to have allowed for the effect of trade and public holidays and weekends that occur within the contract period. However, in calculating the delay caused by the event, is the contractor entitled to this period, even though it encompasses rest days, which are deemed to have been taken into account? The trade holiday was probably taken into consideration within another operation, which, if dependent on the first operation's completion, would be affected as shown in Figure 6.5. The second operation's planned duration before the delaying event was 15.5 calendar days; the delay has reduced it to 9 because there is no longer an intervening holiday within this activity. The overall period for the two operations before the delaying event was 29 calendar days; after the delay event it is 35.5 calendar days, a total delay of 6.5 calendar days.

However, the crucial point is the effect on the completion date. If the second operation was the last operation before the completion date, the effect on the completion date would be the total delay of 6.5 calendar days.

When considering the effect of this delay event, the architect could adopt one of two approaches.

FIGURE 6.4: *Impact of trade holidays falling within delay period*

Days	1	2	3	4	5	6	7	8	9	10	11	12	13	14	15	16	17	18	19	20	21	22	23	24	25	26	27	28	29	30
	M	T	W	T	F	S	S	M	T	W	T	F	S	S	M	T	W	T	F	S	S	M	T	W	T	F	S	S	M	T
Planned operation																														
Trade holiday																														
Delay event																														
Displaced operation																														
Period of delay																														

Primary　　　　　　　　Secondary

FIGURE 6.5: *Trade holidays falling within delay period: impact on dependent operations*

Days	1	2	3	4	5	6	7	8	9	10	11	12	13	14	15	16	17	18	19	20	21	22	23	24	25	26	27	28	29	30	31	32	33	34	35	36	37	38	39
	M	T	W	T	F	S	S	M	T	W	T	F	S	S	M	T	W	T	F	S	S	M	T	W	T	F	S	S	M	T	W	T	F	S	S	M	T	W	T
Planned first operation																																							
Trade holiday																																							
Delay event																																							
Displaced first operation																																							
Period of delay to first operation																																							
Planned second operation																																							
Displaced second operation																																							
Actual delay to completion																																							

- The architect could take the position that the event caused a delay of 5 working days and add these to the end of the contract period as shown in Figure 6.6. The 5 working days become 6.5 calendar days. This is because the contractor is not deemed to have allowed for weekends and trade holidays that occur outside the contract period. If, however, the week following the date for completion was a trade holiday, as in Figure 6.7, the effect would be 13.5 calendar days.
- Alternatively, if the contract programme is sufficiently detailed and considered reasonably accurate, the architect could follow the effect of the delay through the critical path and establish the effect of the delay on that basis.

Given that the effect on the date for completion is 6.5 calendar days in Figures 6.4 and 6.5, does it matter which is the correct analysis? It does, because there has been a change in the calendar periods within which the two operations are being executed as a result of the delay event. The first operation has changed from 13 calendar days to 26.5 calendar days and the second operation from 16 calendar days to 9 calendar days. These changes may have an effect on later events.

If an extension of time has been awarded and, when the contract has been extended by the period of the award, the extended date falls within a trade holiday as in Figures 6.6 and 6.7, the date for completion must be extended beyond the trade holiday by a further calendar week.

The contract, as already stated, does not allow for extensions of time for trade holidays, so why is the trade holiday included in the extension of time? Because, on the same principle as applied to Figure 6.5, a consequential effect of the event is to extend the contract into the trade holiday. It should therefore be included in the event for which the extension of time to the contract period was made.

One problem with the consequential effect of delay occurs if an earlier delay was the fault of the contractor. For example, in Figure 6.6, if the extension had not been given because the delay was the contractor's risk, this would have delayed completion into the period of the trade holiday, a consequential effect of the contractor's own delay.

It is not possible to fix a completion date within the period of a trade holiday, as the contractor will not be working unless special arrangements are made, and it must therefore be placed beyond the trade holiday.

FIGURE 6.6: *Impact of delay: outcome 1 – allowing for weekend*

| Days | 1 | 2 | 3 | 4 | 5 | 6 | 7 | 8 | 9 | 10 | 11 | 12 | 13 | 14 | 15 | 16 | 17 | 18 | 19 | 20 | 21 | 22 | 23 | 24 | 25 | 26 | 27 | 28 | 29 | 30 | 31 | 32 | 33 | 34 | 35 | 36 | 37 | 38 | 39 |
	M	T	W	T	F	S	S	M	T	W	T	F	S	S	M	T	W	T	F	S	S	M	T	W	T	F	S	S	M	T	W	T	F	S	S	M	T	W	T
Planned first operation																																							
Trade holiday																																							
Delay event																																							
Displaced first operation																																							
Period of delay to first operation																																							
Planned second operation																																							
Displaced second operation																																							
Actual delay to completion																																							
Extension of time																																							

FIGURE 6.7: *Impact of delay: outcome 2 – allowing for weekend and trade holiday*

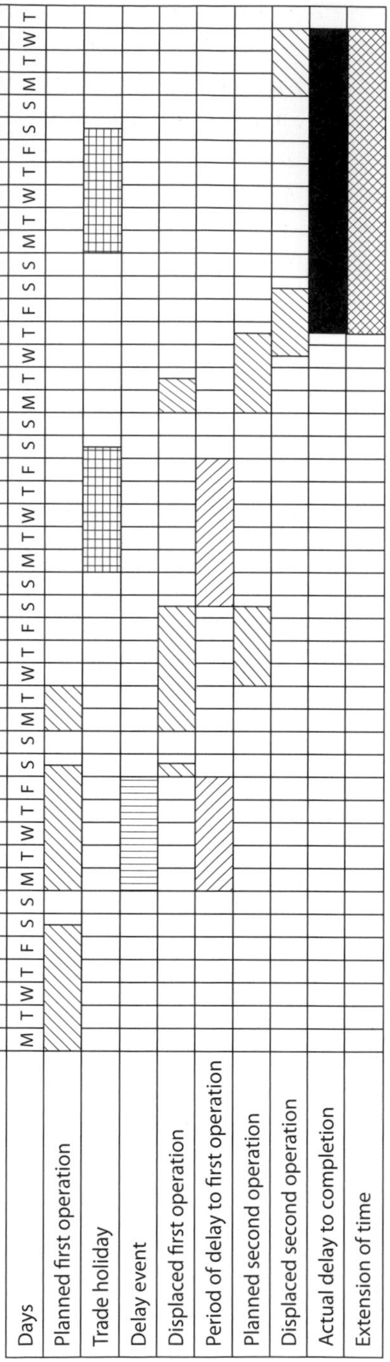

Another consequential effect of a delay event may result from the seasons. For example, where a contract is intended to complete at the end of the summer but delays to the contract put it into the winter weather, sensitive work that the contractor programmed to be carried out during the summer may now have to be carried out during the winter. If further delays occur as a result of the winter working, which are not necessarily events that would give rise to an extension of time, such as exceptionally adverse weather conditions under SBC2005, but merely those that affect progress, these delays will be a consequential effect of the previous delays and should be treated in the same way as the original delay.

In cases like these, the architect must also look at the work carried out at the time of the delay, not the work that, according to the contractor's programme, they would have been carrying out at that time. For example, the work may be delayed because of the contractor's own default, thus causing consequential delay because of exceptionally adverse weather conditions. This, in itself, should not prevent the contractor obtaining an extension of time as a result of that exceptionally adverse weather, although they would still take the risk of delay because of normal bad weather for the time of year.

Individual activity delays

It is important to identify, as accurately as possible, the time when any event that affects progress or causes a delay to an operation occurred. This principle holds true for all events or risks that cause a delay to an operation (see Figure 6.8).

The diagrams in this guide show when the delays occurred and their impact on completion. Figure 6.8 shows a situation that gives rise to delay disputes. There is an original programme, which shows 21.5 activity days. There is an as-built programme, which shows that completion was delayed by 4 days. The as-built programme has 30.5 activity days. For argument's sake let us say that two variations were issued, which the contractor claims caused the delay to completion. Assume that the critical path runs through Brickwork First Operation until day 5 and then drops into Brickwork Second Operation. It then passes into Brickwork Third Operation at day 16 and finally drops into the Next Critical Operation at day 24. The date when the variations were instructed and carried out is crucial to establishing if they had any impact on the critical path. Good record-keeping is vital.

FIGURE 6.8: *Identifying and recording time delays*

Days	1	2	3	4	5	6	7	8	9	10	11	12	13	14	15	16	17	18	19	20	21	22	23	24	25	26	27	28	29	30
	M	T	W	T	F	S	S	M	T	W	T	F	S	S	M	T	W	T	F	S	S	M	T	W	T	F	S	S	M	T
Original programme:																														
Brickwork first operation		▨	▨	▨	▨																									
Brickwork second operation								▨	▨	▨	▨	▨																		
Brickwork third operation																		▨	▨	▨										
Next critical operation																						▨	▨	▨	▨					
As-built programme:																														
Brickwork first operation		▨	▨	▨	▨	▨																								
Brickwork second operation								▨	▨	▨	▨	▨																		
Brickwork third operation															▨	▨	▨	▨	▨	▨										
Next critical operation																							▨	▨	▨	▨	▨		▨	▨
Delay notified																														

Certain events, such as strikes and adverse weather, can be fairly easily identified as, in general, they have an impact on all operations. In other words, progress on site effectively stops. Therefore, provided that records are kept of when the strike or the adverse weather occurred, the period of delay can be assessed.

There is, perhaps, one consequential effect to consider; some consideration may need to be given to a period for getting the site fully up and running.

Variations: additional work

Additional or substituted work does not necessarily cause a delay to an operation. It is the physical and material content that is relevant.

The value of the work involved in the variation may also not be an indicator of delay to the operation. For example, the substitution of gold-plated taps for chromium-plated steel taps will probably increase the value of the work, but it may make no difference to the time taken to execute the operation.

True additional work to an operation, such as increasing the number of taps to fix from 10 to 20, irrespective of gold plating, is always likely to increase the time taken to execute that operation and hence to delay its completion in the absence of 'accelerative' measures such as working overtime or employing additional resources.

Ideally, a variation should be issued in sufficient time for it to be included within the operation that it affects. Thus, its effect is only to increase the time taken to execute the operation as if the variation had been included in the original contract works, and the contractor could have programmed and organised the variation accordingly, irrespective of the contract period.

The omission of work, if instructed in sufficient time, effectively reduces the time to complete an operation.

The objective is to identify when the variation was executed and what impact it had on the operation it affected.

It is sometimes argued that the contractor should increase their resources and so execute the additional work in the same period as the original work. The argument is that the contractor can employ more resources through the increase in the value of the work. However, it should be recognised that labour is not an entirely flexible resource, and so long as the contractor organises their labour resources to carry out the additional work as efficiently as possible, perhaps by reprogramming or reorganising, they have probably discharged their obligations (see *Best endeavours,* below).

Late variations

What if the variation is not issued in sufficient time? In the case of substituted work, this could mean that work already completed has to be taken down and replaced. In the case of additional work it could result in the remobilisation of a subcontractor who has already left the site, and a consequent delay in ordering materials.

The issue to be considered is: when could the work reasonably have been carried out?

Figure 6.9 shows an example of a delay to an operation caused by a late variation to substitute work.

A late variation for additional work could have the same effect, and where the subcontractor involved in the operation has to be remobilised it could place such a delay into a time period of its own. For example, in Figure 6.10 the period for carrying out the variation is 3 calendar days. It could be argued that this is the only period that should be considered for delay. However, if the date shown in Figure 6.10 was the earliest possible time by which the variation could have been executed following its receipt, owing to remobilising and obtaining materials, the delay to the operation is 14 calendar days.

Best endeavours

There is an obligation on the contractor in the JCT forms to use best endeavours to prevent delay (except for MP2005, which imposes a 'reasonable endeavours' obligation, and MW2005). It is expressed in such a way that if the contractor has not used best endeavours, their entitlement to an extension of time may be affected. If, by using best endeavours, a contractor could have prevented delay, the architect is entitled to take that into account in assessing what extension the contractor should be given. This applies whichever party has taken the risk of that delay.

The obligation to use best endeavours was in earlier versions of most of the JCT forms, and the courts have said that this phrase is not the 'next best thing to an

FIGURE 6.9: *Delay caused by a late variation to substitute work*

Days	1	2	3	4	5	6	7	8	9	10	11	12	13	14	15	16	17	18	19	20	21	22	23	24	25	26
	M	T	W	T	F	S	S	M	T	W	T	F	S	S	M	T	W	T	F	S	S	M	T	W	T	F
Planned operation																										
Variation issued																										
Obtain substitute materials																										
Demolish and replace work																										
Delay to operation																										

Date of issue of variation instruction to substitute work

FIGURE 6.10: *Delay caused by a late variation for additional work*

Days	1	2	3	4	5	6	7	8	9	10	11	12	13	14	15	16	17	18	19	20	21	22	23	24	25	26	27	28	29	30	31	32	33
	M	T	W	T	F	S	S	M	T	W	T	F	S	S	M	T	W	T	F	S	S	M	T	W	T	F	S	S	M	T	W	T	F
Planned operation																																	
Variation issued																																	
Remobilise and obtain materials																																	
Execute variation																																	

Date of issue of the variation

absolute obligation or a guarantee' (*Midland Land Reclamation v. Warren Energy* (1997)). It is a duty to do what can reasonably be done in the circumstances. In *Terrell v. Mabie Todd* (1952) the judge said: 'the standard of reasonableness is that of a reasonable and prudent board of directors, acting properly in the interest of their company'.

Other cases make it clear that, in exercising best endeavours, the contractor may need to spend money, and not merely make some kind of token attempt to minimise delay. At the very least, the contractor should re-sequence the works if this could reduce the delay. One recent case, *Rhodia International Holdings Limited v. Huntsman International LLC* (2007), put it like this:

> An obligation to use reasonable endeavours to achieve the aim probably only requires the parties to take one reasonable course, not all of them, whereas an obligation to use best endeavours probably requires a party to take all the reasonable courses he can.

The purpose of an extension of time clause is to maintain the validity of the liquidated damages clause, by relieving the contractor of a liability to liquidated damages for the period of delay that is at the employer's risk. It does not seem reasonable, therefore, to require the contractor to spend more than the amount of those liquidated damages in an attempt to minimise delay. Otherwise, this would negate the purpose of the extension of time clause from the contractor's point of view.

Co-operation between contractor and designers for health and safety purposes is a statutory requirement under the CDM Regulations which applies to all projects, whatever their size or duration. It is also an express obligation for other purposes in some contracts, such as the NEC family of contracts, JCT Constructing Excellence Contract, Framework Agreements and PPC 2000. There is therefore an expectation, whether it is stated in the contract or not, that the contractor will co-operate with the architect in discussing how the delay might be prevented. Many standard forms of contract (but not the JCT forms) provide that if either party, or the architect, believes that there may be a problem in achieving the required time, cost or quality on the project they can call an early warning meeting to discuss how the problem can be overcome.

In making a claim for delay, the contractor should be able to explain how they have used their best endeavours to avoid or reduce delay, and what steps they have taken to do so. This is reinforced by the wording in SBC2005, DB2005 and IC2005, which goes on to require the contractor to do 'all that may reasonably be required to the satisfaction of the Architect to proceed with the Works'. The phrase has not been considered by the courts in a construction context. It could include issues such as re-sequencing. However, the architect must be careful not to make requirements that are in fact variation instructions without consciously deciding to do so.

Making an interim award

Inputting delays into the programme

The award has nothing to do with financial claims. The award process is irrelevant to any financial claim that may be made about the same events.

It is crucial to remember that, unless an event for which the contractor is entitled to an extension of time actually causes a delay to completion of the contract, no extension of time need be considered. There must be a delay to completion of the contract in order to award an extension of time.

The basic principle for analysing the event that is the potential cause of delay to completion is the same whether the programme is computer generated and can be manipulated through the software, or whether it has been manually produced. Any logic links should be carefully checked, as a slight change in logic can have a significant effect. Essentially, the delay is placed or identified in the programme, and it is traced through the critical path for its impact on the completion date (see Figure 6.11). If a programming software package is used, then, in theory, the programme's 'logic' should demonstrate the impact of the event on the completion date.

Common sense should be used. It is not just a case of inputting the data into the programme, pressing a button and expecting an accurate result. If rubbish goes in, the answer will be rubbish. If the answer looks wrong, it might well be wrong. This process does assume that the programme shows a critical path. If a critical path is not shown then the architect should follow what they understand to be the logical sequence of operations to completion to see if the event does cause a delay to the completion date.

A computer model should be treated as an aid and not as the provider of the ultimate answer. Analysis by the architect is always necessary.

FIGURE 6.11: *Impact of delays on the critical path of the project*

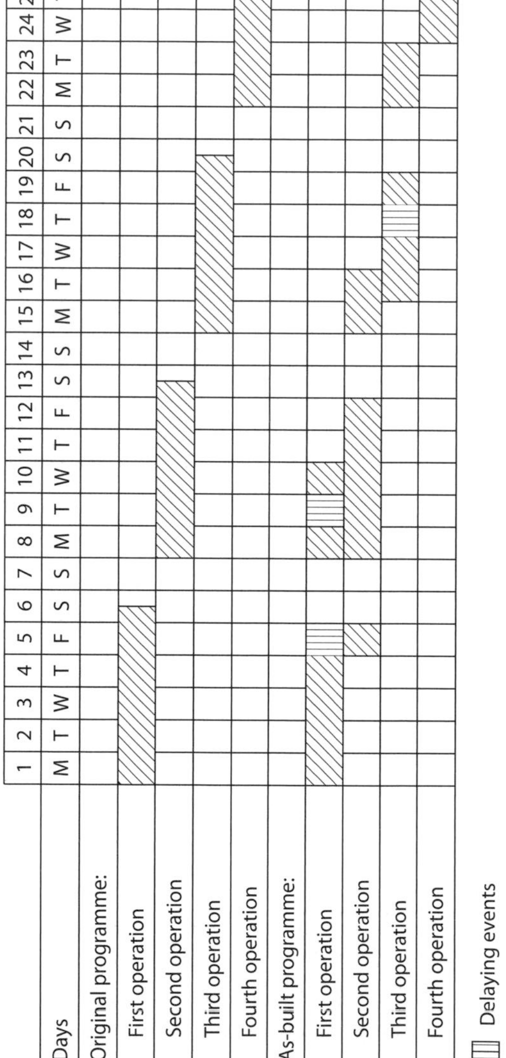

No programme

If, as may be the case on very small contracts, there is no programme, then the process remains the same using the same logic.

Thinking it through logically, a rough hand-drawn programme can assist the process; the architect must consider whether the event would cause a delay to the completion date.

Further assessment after practical completion

After practical completion, the as-built programme can be used to review the extension of time situation. The as-built programme should show the actual delay to the contract and the actual duration of the operations in the programme.

Where the further assessment is carried out manually, the critical path or paths can be established by working back through the operations from practical completion to the start date to establish which operation released the last operation, and so on: the *backward pass*. The same process can then be carried out from the start date, working through the operation which was released by the first operation, and so on: the *forward pass*. The results can be compared and any discrepancies worked through until an as-built critical path or paths can be established.

The delay events not at the risk of the contractor can then be plotted on the as-built programme and their impact on the original completion date can be established: see Figure 6.12.

It is not necessary to plot delays caused by the contractor, as these will be included in the actual duration of the operations; only delays at the contractual risk of the employer need be considered.

Most of the JCT forms (apart from MW2005) provide for a 12-week period after practical completion within which the architect must reassess any extension of time to which the contractor may be entitled, whether they have served a notice of delay or not. (The architect is not permitted to fix a new date earlier than the date for completion.) MP2005 provides for a similar 12-week period, comprising 6 weeks for the provision of information by the contractor and a further 6 weeks for the employer to review and adjust the Completion Date.

FIGURE 6.12: *Delays not at the risk of the contractor: impact on the original completion date*

Days	1 M	2 T	3 W	4 T	5 F	6 S	7 S	8 M	9 T	10 W	11 T	12 F	13 S	14 S	15 M	16 T	17 W	18 T	19 F	20 S	21 S	22 M	23 T	24 W	25 T	26 F	27 S	28 S	29 M	30 T
As-built programme:																														
First operation																														
Second operation																														
Third operation																														
Fourth operation																														

As-built programme with delay events plotted:

First operation																														
Second operation																														
Third operation																														
Fourth operation																														

▨ Delay events

This allows the architect to take an overview of extensions for the whole contract period, in the light of all the information then available. The architect should meet the 12-week period wherever possible, although if the award is made shortly after this period, it is still likely to be valid (*Temloc v. Errill* (1987)).

SUMMARY

- In order to make an assessment of the circumstances of the delay, it is essential to have as accurate a picture as possible of the project, drawn from all the relevant sources of information.
- The differences between calendar and working days, the seasons and the effect of the cycle of a particular operation on the effective working day must all be taken into consideration in the assessment of an extension.
- Strict records of any event that has an impact on any critical path should be maintained to facilitate assessment of the effect on the completion date.
- A variation requiring substituted work may not necessarily cause a delay to an operation if the physical and material content is comparable, whereas a variation issued late will almost invariably affect the completion date.
- The JCT forms place an obligation on the contractor to use best endeavours to prevent any delay.

Section 7
Concurrent delays

In this Section:

- *Concurrency defined*
- *The tortious solution*
- *Assessment where there is concurrency*

Concurrency defined

Concurrent delays are one of the more difficult aspects of delay for an architect to consider when assessing an application for an extension of time. Delays are said to be *concurrent* when they affect the progress of the works at the same time. Often, two different causes of delay are partially concurrent; for example, where the contractor is already being delayed because of a shortage of materials and the work is then affected by exceptionally adverse weather conditions. In that example the contractor will notify delay for the adverse weather, but the question to be decided by the architect is whether the contractor's own delay should be taken into account.

Delays that are partially concurrent are fairly common, and it is unfortunate that the courts have never given a definitive ruling on the way in which an architect should assess what extensions should be granted, and for what reason, when there are two or more competing causes.

The tortious solution

The issue may be argued not as a matter of entitlement under a contract, or as a breach of contract, but also in tort. On that basis, the court in *Stapley v. Gypsum Mines* (1953) held that 'the question must be determined by applying common sense to the facts of each particular case'. If either of the competing causes was a material factor, the party liable for that cause could also be held liable for the whole of the loss.

Example

A television mast collapsed, partly as a result of bad weather but also through negligent design by the subcontractors. The subcontractors' contribution to the failure was less significant than that of the bad weather, but they were held liable in tort for the whole of the loss because their negligence had materially contributed to the collapse (*IBA v. EMI and Anor* (1980)).

There is an old case on concurrency concerning a ship, the *Yorkshire Dale* (1942), which became stranded partly because the navigator had chosen a particular route to avoid enemy submarines, but also because there was an unusual tidal set that had taken the ship too close to the rocks round the Outer Hebrides. The case went to the House of Lords, where it was stated: 'One has to ask oneself what was the effective and predominant cause of the accident that happened, whatever the nature of that accident may be.' Another of the Lords said: 'Each case must be judged in the light of its own facts and by resorting, not to the refinements of the philosophical doctrine of causation, but of the common place tests that the ordinary businessman conversant with such matters would adopt.'

This approach was confirmed in *The Carslogie* (1952). That case concerned a ship that was damaged in a collision. Temporary repairs were effected, and the ship then sailed from Britain to New York, where permanent repairs could be carried out. Owing to heavy weather experienced on that voyage, by the time the ship arrived at New York it was no longer seaworthy, and repairs to rectify the collision damage were carried out at the same time as repairs to make the ship seaworthy again. The court said that the ship that had caused the collision was not responsible for the loss of hire while the repairs were carried out in New York, because the ship would have been out of action anyway as a result of the weather damage. Although the language of effective and predominant causes was not used in that case, the same principles were applied.

The conclusion of this and other cases seems to be that in tort the 'dominant cause' approach is the correct one, to be applied with a certain amount of common sense.

Assessment where there is concurrency

The cases on tort are helpful, but do the same principles apply where an architect is assessing a contractual claim brought under the terms of a construction contract? The JCT forms envisage that delays happen in sequence, rather than at the same time, so the structure of the extension of time clauses is not really geared to dealing with concurrent delays.

Employer delay when contractor already in delay

While the contractor is suffering delay, an event may occur that clearly entitles the contractor to an extension of time. This could be a neutral event for which the employer has taken the risk, such as exceptionally adverse weather. It could even be an employer's delay, such as a variation instruction. In both these situations the architect should not award an extension of time for the employer's delay event unless they consider that the new event has caused or will cause a delay to the contractor additional to the delay already being experienced. The judge in *The Royal Brompton Hospital v. FA Hammond and Ors* (2000) did not consider that this situation was a case of genuine concurrency in any event. However, he did go on to say, later in his judgment, that where the contractor was in delay 'an extension of time could be justified if a contractor was prevented from recovering lost time by the occurrence of a relevant event'. The architect in such a case would need to consider carefully whether the contractor could have recovered lost time, but for the Relevant Event.

The courts have not provided much assistance where there are two or more causes of delay and both employer and contractor need to know what delay is attributable to each of them. In all but the most obvious cases the architect will have to exercise their own judgment, based on what they consider to be fair and reasonable in all the circumstances. For instance, if there has been a delay to the contractor because of a variation instruction, and at the same time a delay because of a failure to grant access, the financial consequences to the contractor will be roughly the same, and the determination of which of the two events was the true cause of delay is of no great significance.

Alternatively, work might not be possible on site for a week due to exceptionally bad weather (at the employer's risk), but during that same week the contractor could experience a labour shortage (at their own risk) which, irrespective of weather conditions, would prevent work from continuing during that week. This example was used by the judge in *Henry Boot v. Malmaison* (1999), where he suggested that if failure to work during that week was likely to delay the works beyond the date for completion and 'if he considers it fair and reasonable to do so', then the architect should award an extension of time and could not refuse to do so on the grounds that the delay would have occurred in any event by reason of the labour shortages. However, that case also confirmed that 'it is impossible to lay down hard and fast rules' and that the question of whether a Relevant Event has caused delay will depend on the facts of each case. In other words, the architect will need to make an assessment based on what is fair and reasonable. This approach was recently endorsed by the Scottish courts in *City Inn Limited v. Shepherd Construction Limited* (1997).

Where there is a delay because of, say, extremely adverse weather conditions, and at the same time a variation instruction is issued, the contractor will (for the purposes of advancing a loss and/or expense claim) want to know the reasons why the architect has given an extension of time, and what time has been allocated to each delay. The architect must say which Relevant Events have been taken into account and what period has been allocated to each Relevant Event when there is more than one involved.

The authors of *Keating on Building Contracts*, one of the leading textbooks, suggest that the 'dominant cause' approach should be modified when applied to the context of concurrent delaying events. They identify a trend towards an analysis which allows the contractor an extension of time where the matter on which they rely has equal 'causative potency' with other delaying events, even if the matter relied on is not the dominant cause in the traditional sense. This analysis seems to have been supported by the judge in the *Malmaison* case in the illustrative example which he gave in his judgment (see above). Although this more 'contractor friendly' approach perhaps reflects the more recent thinking in the analysis of concurrent delay, the architect would be well

FIGURE 7.1: *Two events in parallel that cause a delay*

Days	1	2	3	4	5	6	7	8	9	10	11	12	13	14	15	16	17	18	19	20	21	22	23	24	25	26
	M	T	W	T	F	S	S	M	T	W	T	F	S	S	M	T	W	T	F	S	S	M	T	W	T	F
First operation																										
Delay event 1																										
Delay event 2																										
Second operation																										
Third operation																										
Fourth operation																										
Completion date																										
Impact on completion of delay events																										

FIGURE 7.2: *Two events causing a concurrent delay to completion*

Days	1	2	3	4	5	6	7	8	9	10	11	12	13	14	15	16	17	18	19	20	21	22	23	24	25	26
	M	T	W	T	F	S	S	M	T	W	T	F	S	S	M	T	W	T	F	S	S	M	T	W	T	F
First operation																										
Delay event 1																										
Delay event 2																										
Second operation																										
Third operation																										
Fourth operation																										
Completion date																										
Impact on completion of delay events																										

advised not to lose sight of the obligation to award an extension only when it would, in the architect's opinion, be fair and reasonable to do so.

Some authors have suggested an alternative approach: that of apportioning the loss. This could be achieved by, for instance, an extension being granted for the Relevant Event, but no prolongation costs being awarded. It could be used where a variation is instructed while the contractor is in delay through their own default. This is an interesting suggestion, but is not supported by the wording of the JCT forms. The exception to this is MW2005, which gives the architect the discretion to make an overall judgment as to the extension to be granted, without the need to apportion between different causes of delay. It is worth noting, however, that under MW2005, except for variations, the grounds for extensions of time cannot form the basis of a claim for further payment. It is not, therefore, appropriate simply to adopt the MW2005 approach to assessing extensions of time, where the work is of a more complex nature, and the contractor expects that some grounds for extensions of time will also be the basis of a claim for extra money.

Concurrency can appear in two guises. The first occurs when two events that occur at the same time in parallel cause a delay to completion: see Figure 7.1. This form of concurrency is rare where two distinct events are the cause. The most likely form of this type of concurrency occurs when the contractor complains of information continually being supplied late by the architect, thus causing ongoing delay, and when the architect maintains that the contractor is under-resourced and, as a result, is continually delayed.

The second and more common form of concurrency occurs when two events have the effect of causing a concurrent delay to completion: see Figure 7.2.

The event and the effect can occur at the same time, when the completion date has been passed and no extension has been awarded. Although the case was about 'dotting on', these were the facts in *Balfour Beatty Building Ltd v. Chestermount Properties Ltd* (1993): see Figure 7.3.

FIGURE 7.3: *The Chestermount case*

Completion date																
Contract work and effect of preceding delays																
Variation issued																
Time to complete variation																

> ### *Dotting on*
>
> 'Dotting on' is the name for the principle that in the case of an alteration or modification of the design, quality or quantity of the works, the net delay is to be awarded, not the gross delay. Figure 7.4 sets out the net and the gross. The period of the net delay is added to the completion date.

FIGURE 7.4: *Net and gross delays*

Completion date	
Variation issued	
Time to complete variation	
Gross delay	
Net delay	

The important matter to consider if the issue of concurrency arises is whether both events are actually causing a delay to completion. The examples above, for the purposes of illustration, assume that the 'concurrent events/delays' are causing a delay to completion. In the case of Figure 7.3 it can be argued that this must be the case, because the completion date has been passed. However, analysis of the events may show that there is in fact no concurrency at all but only one cause of delay to completion.

SUMMARY

- Concurrent delays are one of the more difficult aspects of delay for an architect to consider as it is frequently difficult to establish definitively which of two events, for example adverse weather and a shortage of materials, is the true cause of delay.
- If the issue is argued as a tort the 'dominant cause' approach is usually adopted.
- The JCT forms envisage that delays happen in sequence, so concurrent delays pose a particular problem for the extension of time clause.
- It is important to consider whether in the case of apparent concurrency both events are actually causing a delay or if careful analysis will show that there is in fact only one cause of delay to completion.

Section 8
Ethical issues

In this Section:

- *Reasonable skill and care*
- *Extensions of time for late information*
- *Provision of information*
- *Employer's/client's influence*

Reasonable skill and care

As a professional person, the architect has an implied duty to act with reasonable skill and care in carrying out duties in relation to a project. Quite often the form of appointment will set a somewhat higher standard, in which case that will apply. The concept of what constitutes reasonable skill and care has changed over the years, and this means that the decisions in some of the earlier cases where this issue was discussed may not now be followed. For instance, the expectation that architects should not delay the contractor by late production of their design, or by delay in making comments on subcontractors' designs, has become more focused in recent years. An architect should expect to find within the architect's appointment an obligation to have due regard to the timing set out in the construction contract, if not a slightly more onerous obligation in relation to timing. The RIBA Standard Conditions of Appointment for an Architect (CA-S-07-A) provide:

> A2.1.2 The Architect ... performs the Services, so far as reasonably practicable, in accordance with ... any time-scale ... agreed with the client.

An explanation of an architect's duties was given by Judge Seymour in *The Royal Brompton Hospital NHS Trust v. FA Hammond and Ors* (2000):

> The duty of a professional man, generally stated, is not to be right, but to be careful ... the fact that he is in the event proved to be wrong is not, in

itself, any evidence that he has been negligent. His conduct has to be judged having regard to the information available to him, or which ought to have been available to him, at the time he gave his advice or made his decision or did whatever else it is that he did.

Part of the duty to be careful involves a methodical approach to the award of extensions of time. The architect should keep a record of how that decision was reached, for instance, so that it is clear to anyone looking at it subsequently that there was logic behind the decision. In *John Barker Construction Ltd v. London Portman Hotel Ltd* (1996) the judge said that the architect's assessment of an extension of time was fundamentally flawed because:

1. the architect did not carry out a logical and methodical analysis of the impact that certain matters would have on the contractor's programme;
2. the architect made an impressionistic, rather than a calculated, assessment of the time it would take for various items to be carried out;
3. the contractual provisions had been misapplied;
4. some of the allowances made for Relevant Events bore no logical or reasonable relation to the delay caused.

Extensions of time for late information

The architect needs to be aware of time constraints in the construction contract, particularly in relation to the production of design information or clarification. Quite often, at the pre-construction site meeting, the periods will be set down within which the architect and other designers are required to comment on information provided by the contractor or their design subcontractors. If no one else raises this point it is certainly in the architect's interest to do so, as it will provide an appropriate discipline for everyone involved. Having agreed those time scales, the architect must then keep to them. Failure to do so will expose the employer to a claim for an extension of time from the contractor on the ground of late information.

Some employers are much more sensitive to this issue than others. Some employers take the view that if any information is provided late, with the result that the contractor is entitled to an extension of time, this must be the responsibility of one or other of the design team, and they will look to whoever is responsible for compensation. In practice, when information is late, it is often due to a combination of events. This does not protect the architect from ultimate liability, however, if the delay is due to the architect's default in this area.

There is a further factor: the architect is in the unusual position of being, to some extent, judge in their own cause, since as contract administrator the architect has the duty to decide whether an extension of time should be awarded to the contractor, and this will include extensions that are based on the architect's own late information.

An architect faced with this situation must act professionally. It is important to do so for two reasons. First, architecture is a profession, and the architect should therefore act with integrity, even if it may not be in the architect's own personal interest to do so. It is important to remember, of course, that if an architect's award is disputed, the contractor can take the award to adjudication, arbitration or litigation, where it may be overturned. It is likely to be cheaper and more satisfactory for all concerned to deal with applications for extensions as objectively as possible at the beginning. Second, the architect in administering the construction contract is under an obligation to act fairly as between the employer and the contractor. This obligation is implied even if it is not stated expressly. In *Sutcliffe v. Thackrah* (1974) the House of Lords said:

> the building owner and the contractor make their contract on the understanding that in all such [contract administration] matters the architect will act in a fair and unbiased manner and it must therefore be implicit in the owner's contract with the architect that he shall not only exercise due care and skill but also reach such decisions fairly holding the balance between his client and the contractor.

The contractor is entitled to the extensions provided for by the construction contract, even if these may not be directly in the interests of the employer or the architect, because that is the way the construction contract has been structured.

Provision of information

SBC2005 and IC2005 provide that the Information Release Schedule (IRS) can be the basis for the timing of production of information by the architect and other members of the design team.

The process works like this: the use of the IRS is optional. If it is used, the employer must produce the IRS by the date of execution of the construction contract. It is to contain a list of all the further information that the contractor needs, and the dates by which such information is to be provided by the designers.

The contractor is entitled to an extension of time if the information is not provided by the dates on that schedule and the failure to supply the information causes delay. If the IRS is not used, the onus is on the architect to provide the contractor with information when the contractor needs it, in the light of their progress to date, but there is no obligation to provide it earlier than the contractor needs it in order to achieve the completion date.

This is very different from the way in which the clause on late information worked previously. It is no longer a question of the contractor requesting information within a period during which it is reasonable for them to request it, having regard to the progress of the works. There is now either an absolute date for the production of information, set out in the schedule, with which the designers must comply, or the architect must provide information by the date on which the contractor needs it, without knowing what the lead times may be for particular materials, and other relevant factors.

If the architect fails to provide this information, the contractor will be entitled to an extension of time if delay arises for this reason. The architect must make an assessment of the extension of time to which the contractor may be entitled on the basis of the strict interpretation of that clause. The architect is, of course, allowed to consider the other factors that are relevant to an award, such as deciding whether the event in question has actually caused delay, and whether the contractor has used their best endeavours to prevent delay.

It can be difficult for the architect to meet the timetable of the IRS or, if that is not used, to know when information is required by the contractor. This can be managed by the architect either working to the timetable in the schedule, or by agreeing with the contractor in advance what further information is required and by what dates. If, despite that, information is provided late, the architect must award an extension of time on this ground, even if it arises through the architect's own lateness.

Employer's/client's influence

As part of the obligation to act fairly between employer and contractor under the construction contract, the architect must not be influenced improperly by either party in coming to a decision on contract administration issues. This includes a decision on extensions of time. For instance, the employer may be very keen not to grant extensions to the contractor, because this would mean that they would lose some of their liquidated damages. In other cases, the employer may have no particular need for the building on the day on which it is due to be completed because they have not found anyone to occupy it, and they may therefore be interested in encouraging the architect to say the building is not yet practically complete.

Sometimes these influences can be quite subtle and sometimes they can be entirely blatant. The architect must make an assessment of the extension of time to which they believe the contractor is entitled. The architect can inform the employer of the extension that they propose to award, before notifying the contractor, but must be very careful not to be influenced by the employer. If the employer points out a factor that the architect has not taken into consideration, and which is relevant to the assessment of extensions of time, this can be taken into account if appropriate, but the architect cannot simply award a greater or lesser extension because that suits the client.

Similarly, if the employer does not want the architect to give the contractor an extension of time at all, the architect may need to remind the employer that if, in those circumstances, the architect fails to operate the procedure for extensions of time, this could mean that time becomes at large, with all the adverse consequences for the employer described in Section 1, *Does the extension of time clause always apply? Time at large*, page 9. If the employer merely wishes the architect to consider the notice of delay but not award an extension even if the architect thought one was justified, the architect cannot agree to this, for the reasons set out earlier in this section. Even if the reason for the extension is late information from the architect, and the employer threatens to sue the architect, the architect must still grant the extension. Failure to do so puts the employer at risk of a claim from the contractor, which the employer would find it difficult to defend because the architect would have to say, if asked, that they believed that the contractor's claim was justified.

SUMMARY

- The architect has an implied duty to act with reasonable skill and care in carrying out duties in relation to a project, including avoiding causing any delay by late supply of design information or comments on subcontractors' designs. The appointment may expressly require a higher standard than that.
- It is vital to keep an accurate record of how any decision on an award of extension of time was reached, in case of any disputes arising later.
- Architects must act with complete integrity in deciding whether to award an extension of time, even if their own late supply of information is the cause of the delay.
- As part of the obligation to act fairly between employer and contractor under the construction contract, the architect must not be influenced improperly by either party in coming to a decision on extension of time.

Section 9
The NEC provisions for extension of time

In this Section:

- *Basic principles of the NEC*
- *Liquidated damages*
- *Grounds for extensions of time*
- *Notification*
- *Assessment*

Basic principles of the NEC

The NEC contract is different in many material respects from the JCT Suite of Contracts. The contract is administered by a project manager, whose function is to give instructions to the contractor, to assess interim payments and to assess extensions of time and any additional payments that may be due. In this capacity, the project manager does not have any responsibility for the design of the works, or for the quality of workmanship, which is overseen by the supervisor. On a small project, it is not uncommon for the project manager and/or the supervisor also to be a member of the design team.

The project manager is not acting independently of the employer, but is the mouthpiece of the employer. However, the contract provides limits within which the project manager must exercise their functions. If the project manager strays beyond those limits, the contractor is able to claim a compensation event which will entitle them to time and money. Ultimately, the contractor's remedy, if the project manager acts for reasons not stated in the contract, is to refer to adjudication.

The contract aims to require both project manager and contractor to manage the works, largely together, as the project progresses. There are various tools to assist in the management.

The first is the programme, which enables both project manager and contractor to monitor progress on a day-by-day basis by reference to an accepted programme.

In all NEC contracts, the contractor is required to provide a detailed programme. The programme must show the planned sequence of work, dates when information is required, the employer's float, the contractor's float and 'time risk allowances'. Time risk allowances are the times added to specific activities where it is not possible accurately to assess the likely length of a particular activity.

The contractor is entitled to plan to complete the works earlier than the completion date. If the project manager accepts the earlier planned completion in the accepted programme, then the employer, designers, project manager and supervisor are all bound by the dates for them to provide work in order that the earlier completion date can be achieved. If earlier planned completion is provided for in the accepted programme, the period between the planned completion date and the completion date is the contractor's float. This is maintained because, in assessing any extensions of time, the project manager must assess by reference to the planned completion date, thus preserving the period between planned completion and the completion date.

Time risk allowances and other float shown on the programme before the planned completion date will benefit both employer and contractor. Until that float has been exhausted, there will be no effect on the planned completion date.

Once the project manager has accepted the programme, it becomes the accepted programme, and a contract document. It must be updated at regular intervals, the period being laid down in the contract particulars.

The accepted programme thus forms a crucial part in any assessment of extensions of time. If the contractor fails to provide an accepted programme, or fails to update it as required by the contract, they are penalised in the method of assessment of compensation events.

Second, both parties are required to give notice to the other if either becomes aware of something which could delay completion, increase cost or impair performance of the works. These are known as early warnings.

Once an early warning has been given by the contractor or the project manager, if it would be appropriate either party can require a meeting to follow up the warning. The meeting is known as a risk reduction meeting. Other people, such as the designers or the employer, may be invited to attend. The purpose of the meeting is to explore the optimum ways to avoid or reduce the delay or cost implications, or the effect on quality. Solutions must be sought 'that will bring advantage to all those who will be affected' (clause 16.3).

The requirement to give an early warning is given teeth by the method of assessment of time and cost, as detailed later in this chapter (see page 117).

Third, if the contractor is entitled to additional time and cost, these are assessed together, and always during the course of the works. This is to ensure that the effect of delaying events is known quickly and managed as well as possible by the contractor. Because of the regime of dealing with delaying events as they arise, there is no need or provision for a post-practical completion review, as in the JCT contract.

An event which gives rise to an entitlement to time and money for the contractor, that is an event which is at the employer's risk under the contract, is called a compensation event. This section considers in detail what those events are and how the time element of the effects of those events is assessed.

Liquidated damages

The NEC contract makes provision for 'delay damages', that is liquidated damages. The provision is not part of the main contract conditions, but a secondary option, which the employer can elect to exercise if they so choose.

If the option for delay damages has been exercised, damages are payable daily from the contractual completion date until either actual completion or the employer taking over the works. There is no requirement for any specific notice, although if delay damages are to be deducted from a certificate, notification of the amount to be withheld has to be given in accordance with the Housing Grants, Construction and Regeneration Act 1996.

If the completion date is revised after delay damages have been deducted, the employer must repay the delay damages in the next interim payment assessment. The employer is also obliged to pay interest calculated at the rate provided in the contract between the date of payment of the damages and the date of the interim payment assessment when they are certified to be repaid.

If the employer takes over part of the works, the delay damages are reduced. The project manager determines the reduction by assessing the benefit to the employer of taking over that part as a proportion of the benefit to the employer of taking over the whole works. Note that the calculation is by reference to benefit to the employer, not by reference to the value of the works taken over. Thus, for example, if an employer were able to take over the whole of the structure, with only external landscaping outstanding, the benefit to the employer could be almost 100 per cent of the value of taking over the whole of the works.

Grounds for extensions of time

Any event which is at the risk of the employer for time and money is called a compensation event, i.e. it compensates the contractor for any delay or additional cost. In the NEC, all compensation events can potentially lead to additional time and additional money; the two are assessed together. However, for the purposes of this section, only extensions of time will be considered.

All compensation events are listed in clause 60.1 of the contract. They are as follows:

1. The project manager giving an instruction to vary the works (in the language of the NEC contract, to 'change the Works Information'). There are two exceptions:
   • where the change was made to accept a defect for which the contractor was responsible, or
   • where the contractor elects to change the design of any element for which they have design responsibility.
2. The employer fails to provide access to all or any part of the site by the date shown on the accepted programme.
3. The employer fails to provide something they are required to provide by the date shown on the accepted programme. This could apply, for example, to any plant or materials to be provided by the employer.
4. The project manager instructs the contractor to stop working on any element of the work, or not to start on any part of the work. Also, if the project manager changes a key date, this is also a compensation event under clause 60.1(4). A key date is a date nominated by the employer by which

the contractor is to have the works, or part of the works, in a particular condition. For example, part of the works may need to be ready early for specialist fitting out by other contractors.

5. The employer or any other party fails to work within the times shown on the accepted programme, or fails to work within the conditions set out in the works information, or work is carried out on site by others which had not been provided for in the works information.

6. The contract data sets out the time within which the contractor, project manager and supervisor must reply to any communication. Certain clauses of the contract also have specified time limits within which the project manager must respond. If the project manager or supervisor fails to reply to a communication within the stated period, the contractor is entitled to claim a compensation event.

7. The project manager gives an instruction for dealing with an object of historical or other interest found on the site.

8. Either the project manager or the supervisor changes a previous decision which they have made.

9. The project manager withholds an acceptance for a reason not stated in the contract. There are various circumstances in which the project manager is required to give an acceptance, for example to a choice of subcontractor, or to accepting the contractor's programme. The contract provides the parameters within which the project manager can legitimately withhold acceptance. If they refuse acceptance for any other reason, the contractor is entitled to claim a compensation event to recover any additional time or costs caused.

10. If the supervisor instructs the contractor to search for a defect, and no defect is found, a compensation event arises. There is an exception to this. If the search was necessary because the contractor failed to give the supervisor notice before the work was covered up, then the search will not give rise to a compensation event.

11. The supervisor carries out any test or inspection and causes unnecessary delay. All of the tests to establish whether a compensation event has occurred aim to be as objective as possible, but this compensation event does require a subjective judgment by the project manager. To avoid this, the supervisor should estimate the length of testing in advance so that it can be recorded on the accepted programme. That estimate then forms the base for assessing whether any additional delay was 'unnecessary'.

12. Unforeseen physical condition. This can refer to any form of 'physical' condi-
    tion including ground conditions, but excluding weather. The condition
    must be within the site. The contractor takes the risk of any unforeseen
    physical conditions beyond the site.

    The contract aims to make the test of 'unforeseen' as objective and
    detailed as possible to avoid argument. Thus, in order to be 'unforeseen':
    • an experienced contractor would have judged the condition so unlikely to
      arise that it would have been unreasonable to allow for it;
    • the contractor is assumed to have taken into account:
      ◦ site information provided by the employer,
      ◦ publicly available information about the site,
      ◦ information from a physical inspection of the site, and
      ◦ other information which an experienced contractor would reasonably
        have obtained.
    Note that the test is by reference to an experienced contractor, not the parti-
    cular contractor, or even the average contractor.

    When assessing the effect of unforeseen physical conditions, and indeed
    of unusual weather (the next compensation event), the contractor is only
    entitled to time and money for the effect over and above what might
    have been expected by way of physical conditions, or of weather.

    If site information provided by the employer contains any inconsistency or
    ambiguity in relation to physical conditions, the contractor is assumed to
    have taken into account the interpretation more favourable to carrying out
    the works.

13. Exceptional weather conditions experienced at the site will entitle the
    contractor to additional time and money. The contractor is required to
    record the weather measurements set out in the contract data and to
    compare these with the specified, independently recorded weather data. In
    order for the contractor to demonstrate that weather entitles them to a
    compensation event, they must demonstrate that the weather conditions in
    a calendar month, compared to the recorded weather data for that month,
    occur less frequently than once in 10 years. The contractor thus takes the
    risk of weather occurring at least once every 10 years, but also takes the risk
    if freak weather conditions occur at the end of one month and the beginning
    of the next, since assessments are only made by reference to average weather
    during each calendar month. The effect of weather in the standard clause
    60.1(13) compensation event is limited to weather experienced at the site.

If a site could be affected by weather some distance away (for example, heavy rainfall or melting snows in the hills which could cause a river to flood), then the water height of the river at the site should be added to the weather measurements so that any flooding beyond the 10-year occurrence would be a compensation event.

If the works take place over a long distance, such as building a road or pipeline, it would be necessary to specify measurement of weather, and records of weather data, in more than one place.

14. An employer's risk occurs. The employer's risks are listed in clause 80.1 of the contract. They are:
    - claims, proceedings, compensation or costs due to use or occupation of the site by the works, which is an unavoidable result of the works;
    - negligence, breach of statutory duty or other act by the employer or persons for whom the employer is responsible;
    - a fault in the employer's design;
    - loss or damage to plant and materials provided by the employer prior to the contractor accepting them;
    - loss due to risks not covered by normal all-risks insurance (i.e., war, etc.), strikes and radioactive contamination;
    - loss or damage to the works after the employer has taken them over or after termination.

    It is also possible for the contract data to list other matters which it is agreed will be at the employer's risk.

15. The employer takes over part of the works before the contractual completion date, and before completion of the works, unless this was provided for in the works information. In the language of the JCT contracts, this would be partial possession but, unlike the JCT, in the NEC contract the employer does not require the contractor to consent to take over part. If the contractor is caused cost or delay by the taking over, they are entitled to claim a compensation event.

16. The employer fails to provide any materials, facilities and samples for tests and inspections that they are required to provide in accordance with the works information.

17. The project manager notifies a correction to an assumption of an earlier compensation event. As detailed below, once compensation events are evaluated for time and money, the result is final and the time and cost implications of a compensation event are not revisited. There is one exception to

this. Where the effect of a compensation event is too uncertain to expect either employer or contractor to be bound by an early assessment of it, the project manager requests the contractor to make various assumptions and to base the quotation on those assumptions. For example, there might be an assumption that certain materials could be procured within one month. If the project manager's assumption subsequently turns out to be wrong, it is dealt with by the contractor advising a new compensation event under this clause 60.1(17).

18. Any breach of the contract by the employer not covered by any other compensation event. In a contract, the employer cannot rely on a liquidated damages clause if the employer's own act has prevented completion. However, a project manager cannot grant an extension of time to preserve the right to claim liquidated damages unless the contract specifically allows them to grant an extension for that reason. To prevent any possibility that time might be at large because of an employer's breach for which the project manager cannot grant an extension of time, this 'catch all' paragraph has been included.

19. Any event which stops the contractor completing the works or stops the contractor completing by the date shown on the accepted programme, which neither party could have prevented. This clause was added in the third edition of the NEC in order to provide a form of force majeure and also to cover the English legal doctrine of frustration. However, unlike either force majeure or frustration, under the NEC if the contractor is prevented from completing the works, it is the employer who carries the risk of any additional time or money incurred by the contractor as a result. Note that the clause requires that the event 'stops' the contractor. It is not sufficient that it merely causes a delay or makes completion more difficult. The event must stop completion of the works by any reasonable means.

If using the NEC contract, it is necessary to decide at the outset which main option will be selected – A, B, C, D or E. These options deal with different methods of payment. Options A and B are fixed price, Options C and D are target price and Option E is a reimbursable contract. Option F is a management contract. One of the results of adopting Options B and D is that they contain additional compensation events.

Option B is a fixed price contract based on a bill of quantities. Option D is a target price contract where the price is fixed by reference to a bill of quantities. If the quantity of work done is more than the quantity stated in the bills of quantities, no compensation event normally arises because the contractor is paid on the basis of measured work completed.

There are three additional compensation events arising out of the use of bills of quantities. By clause 60.4, in both options, the contractor is entitled to a compensation event if there is a difference between the final total quantity of the work done and the quantity stated for an item in the bill of quantities, but only if:

• the difference does not result from a change to the works information (which would be a compensation event under clause 60.1(1)), and
• the difference causes the defined cost per unit of quantity to change, and
• the original rate for the item in the bill multiplied by the final quantity of work done is more than 0.5 per cent of the total of the prices at the contract date.

The effect of this compensation event is that the contractor takes the risk of changes in quantity and rate which have only a minor impact, i.e. less than 0.5 per cent of the original contract price.

A difference between the quantity stated in the bill and the final quantity of work done which causes delay to completion or delays the contractor meeting a key date is a separate compensation event under clause 60.5.

If there is a mistake in the bill of quantities in describing an item in accordance with the method of measurement being used, or there are ambiguities or inconsistencies, the project manager issues instructions to correct them. Each such correction is a compensation event under clause 60.6. Where the project manager corrects a mistake due to an inconsistency between the bill of quantities and some other document, for the purposes of assessing the effect of the compensation event, the contractor is assumed to have taken the bill of quantities as correct.

To use the NEC, it is essential that one of the main options is selected. In addition, there is a list of secondary option clauses which can be included at the option of the employer. Some of the secondary option clauses provide additional compensation events.

Option X2 provides that if there is a change in the law after the contract date, this will constitute a compensation event. If Option X2 is not used, the contractor takes the risk of statutory charges.

Option X14 provides for advanced payment to the contractor. If this option is selected, but the employer delays in making the advanced payment, then that delay is a compensation event.

Option X15 provides the ability to limit the contractor's liability for design to one of reasonable skill and care. Under the standard clauses, the contractor's liability for design is absolute fitness for purpose. If the contractor is requested to correct a design defect for which they are not liable, because Option X15 applies and they can demonstrate that they have exercised reasonable skill and care, then that correction of the design is a compensation event.

The NEC has been written on the basis that it can be used internationally. The standard clauses therefore do not totally comply with the Housing Grants, Construction and Regeneration Act 1996, which applies to most construction contracts in the UK. If that Act applies, then it is compulsory to adopt secondary option Y(UK)2. That secondary option includes an additional compensation event at clause Y2.4. This provides that if the contractor exercises their right under the Act to suspend performance due to non-payment, that is a compensation event.

It is also possible for additional compensation events to be listed in the contract data. If this is done, it is important to describe the compensation event as exactly, and as objectively, as possible. For example:

> Work is stopped due to use of the site by the employer on more than X occasions in Y months.

Notification of compensation events

The philosophy of the NEC is that compensation events are dealt with as soon as possible, and with finality. To that end, the notification requirements are strict, although more relaxed in the current third edition than in the previous two editions.

In the third edition, for the first time, an obligation is placed on the project manager to notify certain compensation events. Where a compensation event arises from either the project manager or the supervisor giving an instruction, or changing an earlier decision, then it is the project manager who notifies the contractor that it is, or could be, a compensation event at the same time as giving the instruction or changing the earlier decision.

The project manager's obligation to notify would apply to compensation events under the following clauses: 60.1(1) – instructions to change the works information; 60.1(4) – an instruction to stop work; 60.1(7) – an instruction to deal with an object of historical interest; 60.1(8) – changing a previous decision; 60.1(10) – the supervisor requesting a search for a defect; 60.1(15) – take-over of part of the works; and 60.1(17) – the project manager notifying a correction to a previous assumption.

If the project manager is obliged under clause 61.1 to notify a compensation event but fails to do so, there is no time limit for the contractor to notify one of those compensation events. The contractor can thus notify a compensation event under any of the clauses listed in the above paragraph effectively at any time prior to completion.

Given the emphasis in the NEC on both contractor and employer being up to date with regard to knowledge of the programme, the budget and payment of costs, it is a great burden on the project manager to ensure that they notify those compensation events which arise from instructions emanating from the project manager or the supervisor.

For all other compensation events listed in clause 60.1, the onus is on the contractor to notify. The time limits for the contractor to notify are strict. If they fail to notify within 8 weeks of becoming aware of the event, they lose any right to claim either additional time or additional cost or an amendment to a key date (clause 61.3).

Where the contractor has notified a compensation event, the project manager must notify their decision within 1 week, or a longer period if the contractor has agreed, whether or not the event is a compensation event. If the project manager fails to give any notification within 2 weeks, then their silence is deemed to be acceptance that a compensation event has occurred.

The project manager's response to the notification of a compensation event by the contractor is either acceptance that the compensation event has occurred or a decision that no compensation event has occurred because:

• the event arises from the fault of the contractor. The simple fact of the occurrence of an event listed in clause 60.1 is not sufficient to constitute a compensation event; the project manager must also be satisfied that the event did not occur as a result of the contractor's fault;

- the event has not happened and is not expected to happen;
- the event will have no effect on either defined cost or completion or meeting a key date;
- the event is not one of the compensation events stated in clause 60.1.

Agreement that a compensation event has occurred can thus arise in three circumstances. The first is where the project manager has notified the contractor of a compensation event arising out of the project manager's instructions; the second is where the contractor has notified a compensation event and the project manager has confirmed that a compensation event has arisen; and the third is where the contractor has notified a compensation event and the project manager has failed to respond at all within 2 weeks of the notification. In each of the three situations, the procedure which follows is the same.

The procedure is that the contractor is required to provide a quotation for the compensation event. The quotation consists of both a revised programme to demonstrate the delaying effect on completion and revised contract prices to demonstrate additional costs.

The contractor must submit their quotation within 3 weeks of being instructed to do so by the project manager. The project manager must then reply within 2 weeks. However, both these time limits can be extended by agreement between the project manager and contractor, but only before the contractual time period has elapsed. If numerous compensation events are occurring, given the time and cost of preparing quotations, there is no objection to the project manager agreeing to 'roll up' several compensation events to be included in one proposed new programme quotation.

The project manager's reply to a quotation can be:

- acceptance of the quotation;
- an instruction to submit a revised quotation, for example because it does not contain all the information the contract requires it to contain;
- notification that the project manager will be making their own assessment.

If the contractor is required to submit a revised quotation, the project manager is obliged to explain their reasons for the requirement. The contractor has a further 3 weeks in which to submit the revised quotation. One of the reasons for requiring the project manager to justify putting the contractor to the expense of an additional quotation is that, on the fixed price Options A and B, the contractor is not paid the cost of preparing quotations; the cost is deemed to be included in the contractor's fee percentage. It would therefore be unfair to burden the contractor with unnecessary quotation costs.

If the project manager fails to reply to a quotation within the time allowed, the contractor may:

- notify the project manager of the failure; and
- if more than one quotation was submitted for the compensation event, notify the one the contractor proposes should be accepted.

If the project manager fails to reply to this notification within 2 weeks, the contractor's notification is treated as acceptance of the quotation.

This provision, and the provision for deeming a compensation event where the project manager fails to respond to the initial notification, is to safeguard against the machinery of the contract breaking down through the failure of the project manager.

Assessment

Completion in the NEC contract is defined as completion of all the work which the works information states must be complete by the completion date, plus correction of all known defects which would prevent the employer from using the works. The definition is therefore more fluid than the concept of 'practical' or 'substantial' completion. It is necessary to check the requirements for completion set out in the works information before the completion date can be confirmed. For example, the contractor may have to provide operation and maintenance manuals, collateral warranties, training or as-built drawings before completion is achieved.

The assessment of a compensation event is a forecast of the delay to the completion date and the delay to any key dates shown on the accepted programme. The quotation also, of course, includes the effect on the cost of the works, but that is not the subject of this section.

Note that the assessment is always made by reference to the planned completion date and the completion date. The extension of time is not calculated as a period from the start date. The response to a compensation event quotation is always a new date for completion, not a period of time of extension.

The completion date, and any key date, is never brought forward as the result of a compensation event, even in circumstances where the prices may be reduced. The only circumstances in which the completion date can be made earlier is where the contractor has provided a quotation for acceleration of the works, and the project manager has accepted it (clause 36).

In preparing the contract programme, the contractor is entitled to show planned completion at an earlier date than the completion date. If they have done so, then the delay is assessed as the delay to planned completion. For example (see Figure 9.1):

1. The contractor plans to complete two weeks earlier than the completion date.
2. A compensation event occurs which causes 1 week's delay.
3. Adding 1 week to the planned completion date would not in fact delay completion, but it would reduce the period between planned completion and the completion date by 1 week.
4. Under the NEC, the period between planned completion and the completion date is float which is owned by the contractor.
5. Therefore, even though the completion date will not be delayed, the contractor is entitled to 1 week's extension of time because planned completion will be delayed.

If the contractor has failed to give an early warning of a compensation event which an experienced contractor could have given, then the effect on the completion date is assessed on the basis that an early warning had been given. This method of assessment only applies if the project manager has notified the contractor at the time when the contractor requests a quotation that the quotation must be based on the assumption that an early warning was given.

The extension of time is also assessed on the assumption that the contractor reacts promptly and competently to the compensation event.

When revising the programme in order to demonstrate the effect on planned completion and the completion date, the contractor is entitled to take into account risk allowances for risks which have a significant chance of occurring and which are at the contractor's risk. For example, if the effect of delay was to move the period of crane operations from July to October, there would be a greater risk of delay to crane operations in October due to a greater likelihood of high winds. The incidence of high winds in October is unlikely to be a

FIGURE 9.1: *Contract programme showing planned and actual completion dates*

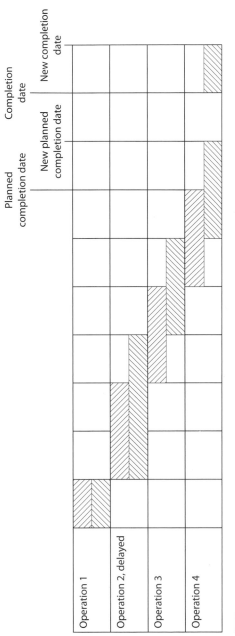

compensation event under clause 60.1(13), so the contractor will need to allow more time for the crane operations being carried out in October.

If the delay to the completion date has been caused by a change to the works information which was to resolve an ambiguity or inconsistency, the contractor is assumed to have taken into account the more favourable interpretation of the works information in the original accepted programme.

Before requesting the quotation, the project manager may discuss with the contractor various ways of dealing with the compensation event. If one favoured solution is reached, then the project manager will instruct that the quotation is provided on that basis. However, it may be that the employer wishes to assess the effect on the completion date of more than one method of dealing with the compensation event. For instance, the employer may want to weigh up the additional costs of acceleration against the costs of delay to the completion date. In those circumstances, the project manager is entitled to ask the contractor to submit quotations on two or more different bases to enable the project manager, on the employer's behalf, to select the quote which best suits the employer.

Assessment by the project manager

There are certain circumstances where the project manager is entitled to assess the programme element of a compensation event. These circumstances are:

- if there is no accepted programme at the time of the quotation, or
- if the contractor has not submitted a revised programme in accordance with the requirements of the contract.

The project manager notifies the contractor that they intend to assess the compensation event and explains their reasons. The project manager is required to submit their quotation in the same period as allowed for the contractor – 3 weeks – and to provide the same details in the quotation as if the contractor had provided it.

If the contractor has submitted a quotation but the project manager notifies their intention to prepare the quote personally and then fails to do so, the contractor can provide notification of the project manager's failure. If the project manager does not reply within a further 2 weeks, then the contractor's quotation will be accepted.

The purpose of making provision for the project manager to carry out assessments in certain circumstances is to incentivise the contractor to prepare an accepted programme and to revise it thereafter in accordance with the contract rather than suffer the disadvantage of having the project manager assess compensation events.

Concurrent delays

In the NEC, all compensation events are compensated by both time and money, unlike the JCT contracts where only certain of the employer's risks under the contract entitle the contractor to additional costs as well as to extensions of time. As a result, under the NEC, there is no need for either party to differentiate between different causes of delay.

Concurrent delays are not specifically referred to in the NEC, but are effectively managed by the need for an up-to-date, accurate accepted programme. The accepted programme must show delays which are at the contractor's risk as well as delays caused by compensation events. The accepted programme should demonstrate actual progress to date and planned progress. It will also show delays due to compensation events, and the current completion date, as well as delays due to the contractor and therefore, potentially, delays beyond the completion date.

The project manager is required to assess the delay caused by a compensation event by reference to actual progress and actual planned progress to calculate the effect on the completion date. This means that if the contractor has caused a delay beyond the completion date, and a compensation event subsequently occurs, the effect of extending the completion date could reduce the contractor's culpable delay period. This would happen if the delay caused by the compensation event was concurrent with the delay caused by the contractor.

Finality

Once the project manager has accepted the contractor's quotation, the extension to the completion date which formed part of the quotation is never revisited or revised. There is one exception to this, where the project manager has instructed the contractor to provide the quote on the basis of a particular assumption and that assumption later turns out to be incorrect. In those circumstances, a separate compensation event is notified but, in reality, the effect on the programme of the initial compensation event is revised.

The assessment of a compensation event is not later revised even if it is shown by recorded information to have been wrong. For example, if the contractor has forecast a delay to planned completion of 2 weeks but is actually able to minimise the delay to 1 week, the extension of time is not revised. There are good reasons for this. The intention is to motivate the contractor to manage the compensation event as well as possible. If the contractor is able to minimise the delay, that is likely to be a benefit both to the contractor and to the employer.

The second reason for not revisiting extensions of time is to provide certainty, both to the contractor and the employer, of the accepted programme, the accepted completion date and the price for the works.

The compensation event procedure does leave open various areas where there will be room for dispute. These include the situations where:

- the project manager fails to accept that an event is a compensation event after notification by the contractor;
- the project manager refuses to accept a quotation of the contractor; or
- the contractor refuses to accept a quotation provided by the project manager.

In all these instances, the remedy is to go to adjudication. It is submitted that, as a result of the dispute procedure, the project manager is incentivised to provide reasonable decisions in order to avoid either the wrath of the employer or frequent adjudications. Equally, the contractor is incentivised to provide reasonable and compliant quotations in order to avoid having the project manager assess the compensation events and/or having to go to adjudication over unacceptable quotations from the project manager.

SUMMARY

Basic principles of the NEC

- The NEC aims to be a contract providing, and enforcing, management tools for the project manager and contractor jointly to manage the construction process, the most important being:
  - very detailed, up-to-date programme requirements;
  - an obligation to give early warnings of matters which could affect time, cost or quality;
  - immediate and prompt assessment of time and cost due to the contractor arising out of events which are at the employer's risk under the contract.

Grounds for extensions of time

- Events at the risk of the employer – compensation events – are to be found:
  - in the core clauses of the contract at clause 60.1;
  - in main Options B and D at clauses 60.4 to 60.6;
  - in secondary Option clauses X2.1, X14.3, X15.2 and Y2.4;
  - in the Contract Data, part one, if the employer has agreed to additional compensation events.

Notification of compensation events

- Either the project manager notifies a compensation event when giving an instruction or the contractor notifies a compensation event.
- The contractor's notification must be within 8 weeks of the event, otherwise it is time barred.
- The project manager must respond to the contractor's notification within 1 week.
- The contractor must provide a quotation for the compensation event within 3 weeks of the notification or the response from the project manager, consisting of a revised programme and revised contract prices.
- The project manager must respond to the quotation within 2 weeks.
- If the contractor is obliged to revise the quotation, or the project manager assesses the compensation event, a further 3 weeks is allowed.

Assessment

- The delay caused by a compensation event is assessed as a revision to the contractor's planned completion date, which will in turn revise the completion date.
- Float prior to planned completion is for the benefit of both contractor and employer.
- Float between the planned completion date and the completion date belongs to the contractor.
- The revision to the programme is assessed on the basis that the contractor gave an early warning and the contractor reacted promptly and competently to the compensation event.
- The project manager is entitled to assess the programme revision personally if the contractor has not provided an accepted programme or not revised the programme in accordance with the contract.
- The assessment of delay caused by a compensation event is final and is not later revised if it proves to have been incorrect.

Glossary

Cause and effect

A cause is the event that gives rise to the alleged delay. The effect is the alleged period of delay that the event causes. There must be a demonstrable link between the two.

Completion date

The date for completion (see below) as it may have been extended under the contract.

Critical path

The sequence of operations through a project network from start to finish, the sum of whose durations determines the overall project duration. See page 58 for more detail.

Critical path network

The process of deducing the critical operations in a programme by tracing the logical sequence of tasks that directly affect the date of project completion.

Date for completion

The date stated in the contract when practical completion is to be achieved.

DB2005

The JCT Design and Build Contract 2005 edition.

Deferring possession

Under the JCT forms, apart from MW2005, the employer is entitled to defer the contractor's possession of the site for up to 6 weeks beyond the contractual date of possession.

Dotting on

This is the name for the principle that in the case of an alteration or modification of the design, quality or quantity of the works, the net delay is to be awarded, not the gross delay.

IC2005

The JCT Intermediate Building Contract 2005 edition, with or without contractor's design.

IRS

Information release schedule.

JCT forms

DB2005, IC2005, MP2005, MW2005 and SBC2005.

Liquidated damages

These are also sometimes known as liquidated and ascertained damages. Damages are the compensation payable to someone for a civil wrong, as opposed to a criminal wrong, for which a different system applies. Damages are usually, but not always, in the form of money. They are called 'liquidated' if the amount is either set out in the contract or can be calculated without the need for a decision by someone such as a judge on how the calculation should be carried out. Damages are said to be unliquidated when the court needs to decide how much loss has been suffered as a result of the wrong.

Damages for the contractor's delay in achieving practical completion are a common example of liquidated damages, because they are usually expressed as £x per week or per day. Unliquidated damages will be payable if there is, say, a defect in design or workmanship and the employer has had to pay for the work to be put right. The court or an arbitrator will decide the amount of those damages, based on evidence about the amount spent by the employer, but will also take into account other aspects such as foreseeability of loss.

MP2005

The JCT Major Project Construction Contract 2005 edition.

MW2005

The JCT Minor Works Building Contract 2005 edition, with or without contractor's design.

Repudiation
A party behaving in a way that shows they no longer intend to be bound by the contract. If the 'innocent' party accepts the repudiation, they are relieved of the duty to carry out their future obligations under the contract, and can recover damages from the repudiating party.

SBC2005
The JCT Standard Building Contract 2005 edition, with or without quantities or with approximate quantities, and with or without contractor's design.

Specified perils
'Fire, lightning, explosion, storm, tempest, flood, bursting or overflowing of water tanks, apparatus or pipes, earthquake, aircraft and other aerial devices or articles dropped therefrom, riot and civil commotion, but excluding Excepted Risks' (radioactivity or pressure waves from supersonic aircraft, etc.) (SBC2005).

Time of the essence
Making 'time of the essence' in a contract means that if the contractor fails to complete on time the employer can treat the contract as being discharged and sue for damages.

Tort
A wrong done by one person or organisation to another which the law recognises as giving rise to a civil remedy in the court, even if the parties are not in contract with each other.

Table of cases

Midland Land Reclamation Ltd v. Warrens Energy Ltd (1997) reported on Lawtel at www.lawtel.co.uk ref. LTL 8/9/97

Multiplex Constructions (UK) Limited v. Honeywell Control Systems Limited (No. 2) (2007) BLR 195

Peak Construction (Liverpool) Ltd v. McKinney Foundations Ltd (1970) 1 BLR 111

Percy Bilton Ltd v. GLC (1982) 17 and 20 BLR 1

Pigott Foundations Ltd v. Shepherd Construction Ltd (1993) 67 BLR 48

Reinwood Ltd v. L Brown & Sons Ltd [2008] UKHL 12 reported on Lawtel at www.lawtel.co.uk ref. LTL 21/2/2008 (Unreported elsewhere)

Rhodia International Holdings Limited v. Huntsman International LLC (2007) 1 CLC 59

Scottish Special Housing Association v. Wimpey Construction UK Ltd (1986) 2 WLR 995

Serck Controls v. Drake & Scull Engineering Ltd (2000) 73 Con LR 100

Shawton Engineering Limited v. (1) DGP International Limited (t/a Design Group Partnership) and Others (2006) BLR 1

Simplex Concrete Piles Ltd v. London Borough of St Pancras (1958) 14 BLR 80

Stapley v. Gypsum Mines (1953) AC 663

Sutcliffe v. Thackrah (1974) AC 727

Temloc Ltd v. Errill Properties Ltd (1987) 39 BLR 30

Terrell v. Mabie Todd & Co. Ltd (1952) 69 RPC 234

Carslogie Steamship Co. Ltd v Royal Norwegian Government [1952] AC 292

The National Trust v. Haden Young Ltd (1994) 72 BLR 1

The Royal Brompton Hospital NHS Trust v. FA Hammond and Ors (2000) AER(D) 2342

Walter Lawrence & Son Ltd v. Commercial Union Properties (UK) Ltd (1984) 4 Con LR 37

Yorkshire Dale Steamship Co. Ltd. v. Minister of War Transport [1942] AC 691

Bibliography and websites

Bibliography

Delay and Disruption in Construction Contracts, K. Pickavance, 2nd edition, LLP, London (2000)

Keating on Building Contracts, S. Furst and V. Ramsey, 7th edition, Sweet & Maxwell, London (2001)

Liquidated Damages and Extensions of Time, B. Eggleston, 2nd edition, Blackwell Science, Oxford (1997)

Useful websites

Software

www.primavera.com

www.microsoft.com

www.astadev.com

Project management organisations

Project Management Institute (US-based project management organisation): www.pmi.org

Association for Project Management (UK-based project management organisation): www.apm.org.uk

Index